CW01020955

Because we are magical women,
born of magical women,
who are born of magical women,
we celebrate your magic.

PEARL CLEAGE, *WE SPEAK YOUR NAMES*

First published in the United Kingdom in 2014 by Rocket 88,
an imprint of Essential Works Limited
29 Clerkenwell Green, London ECIR ODU

This hardback edition published in 2015 by Rocket 88,
an imprint of Essential Works Limited.

Publishers: John Conway, Mal Peachey
Art Director: Michael Gray
Editors: Rose Fox, Fiona Screen, Beth Thomas

ISBN: 9781906615901

Printed in China by Imago

vintageblackglamour.com
vintageblackglamourbook.com
rocket88books.com

VINTAGE **BLACK** GLAMOUR

NICHELLE GAINER

CONTENTS

Nina Simone backstage in Pittsburgh by legendary photographer Charles "Teenie" Harris, circa 1965.

A DIVA IN THE FAMILY

"The sexiest Salome since red-haired Ljuba Welitch."

***TIME*, JULY 14, 1961**

Margaret Tynes (b. 1919) on September 29, 1959 by Carl Van Vechten.

I WAS AT THE SCHOMBURG CENTER for Research in Black Culture in Harlem one afternoon in 2002 when I came across a picture of a stylist doing the hair of a beautiful woman in a sleeveless shift and pearls. I was at there to do some research on a novel I am writing about three friends who meet as Negro beauty contestants in the 1950s. The novel idea was inspired by one of my aunts, Mildred Taylor, who modeled and competed in Negro beauty contests in the 1950s. When she told me that she competed in a national pageant in Indiana, just before she got married, I went straight to the library to see if I could find any pictures of her or the event. I was happy to find a few things in the historic *New Jersey Afro-American* at the Newark Public Library, so I decided to try my luck scouring through some of the old black magazines like *Jet*, *Tan*, *Hue*, and *Our World*. I was stunned to see lots of black starlets—breathlessly covered the way young stars are today in magazines like *Us Weekly* or popular celebrity websites and blogs. I knew about Dorothy Dandridge and Lena Horne, of course, but who knew that there were so many other Negro starlets nipping at their heels?

The picture that caught my eye that afternoon at the Schomburg was clearly taken for publicity purposes, perhaps for a profile, and I was interested in shaping one of my characters, at least in part, after Rose Morgan (1912–2008), the stylist in the photo. Although she is often best remembered for having once been married to boxing legend Joe Louis, Ms. Morgan was a trailblazing entrepreneur who owned the Rose-Meta House of Beauty, one of the first full-service salons for black women in the country. Ms. Morgan also went on to help found the Freedom National Bank in 1965. I was excited to learn more about Ms. Morgan, but it was her client who turned out to be my main interest that day, my aunt Margaret Tynes. I remembered her primarily from a family reunion I attended as a teenager in the late 1980s in Smithfield, Virginia. She was memorable because she was prominently featured in the reunion souvenir booklet that detailed our family history dating back to 1802. Along with several 19th-century poets, writers, and artists in the history of our family, there were pages upon pages of Margaret's photographs, concert programs, and album covers. Just before she settled back in the United States after the death of her husband, the architect and designer Hans von Klier, she made a stop in Greensboro, North Carolina to donate her papers and memorabilia to her undergraduate alma mater, North Carolina A&T State University. "I have had letters from people who said they were cured from hearing me sing or hearing me laugh," she told a reporter for the *Greensboro News & Record* during a visit to the campus. "All I know is I have had a great life," she said. "I have been guarded and guided."

Like many black female performers of her era, Margaret was multi-faceted: well-educated, well-traveled, and multi-lingual. On the one hand, she was raised as a child

Margaret Tynes, Duke Ellington, and Joya Sherrill in a publicity still from the 1957 CBS television special based on Mr. Ellington's jazz suite, *A Drum Is a Woman.*

of privilege, college-educated in the American South at a time when most black women were undereducated and underemployed. She graduated from a historically black college, North Carolina A&T State University, and joined the sorority Alpha Kappa Alpha. But her entertainment career guaranteed that she would not necessarily continue on that trajectory. With one foot firmly planted in the black middle class, Margaret placed the other foot in the world of black entertainment: trying different things, not being limited by the rules of either milieu—what people "normally" did. She tried jazz, theater, opera, and classical, and appeared on television. On her way to Europe in the early 1960s, she met the man who would be her husband of 40 years at the airport; she would have her greatest and best-known professional success as Salome under Luchino Visconti's direction at the famed Spoleto Festival of the Two Worlds in Italy. I was most intrigued by her connections to an American giant: Duke Ellington. People who knew him well knew that early morning phone calls were customary for Mr. Ellington. The late record producer and author Irving Townsend told a story about Ellington's famously nocturnal ways. "We knew that every now and then the phone would ring between 6 p.m. and 6 a.m. and a dark, sleepy voice would say, 'Good morning. Did I wake you? I'm so sorry. What time is it anyway?' " My aunt told me a similar story one afternoon over lunch. "Normally, I was in bed by ten, but one night at about three-thirty in the morning, I pick up the telephone and hear 'Margaret Tynes, this is Duke Ellington.' I answered 'Yes, and I'm the President of the United States' and hung up! Then, he calls right back and says 'Don't hang up! This is the big brother of Ruth Ellington, one of your best friends' and that's when I knew."

Ruth Ellington Boatwright (1915–2004), like Margaret, was an alumna of Columbia University, where she earned a degree in biology. She was also sixteen years younger than her brother and he was famously protective of her. Ruth, for her part, looked out for her big brother as the president of his publishing company. According to Margaret, Ruth never told her that she had given a recommendation to her famous brother, but of course, Margaret didn't mind. Even when it meant having to record in the wee hours of the morning. *A Drum Is a Woman* comes from a long line of signature jazz suites that combined urbane sophistication with "primitive" elements. Ellington always had an interest in highlighting the African roots of black music and his "Black and Tan Fantasy" (1927) and "Black, Brown and Beige" (1943) were sometimes called "jungle style" pieces. He told *Fortune* magazine in 1933, "I have revisited the history of my people trying to express it through rhythm." In 1954, he told *Downbeat* magazine about plans for his musical narrative history of the Negro and, on May 8, 1957, CBS's *U.S. Steel Hour* presented *A Drum Is a Woman* as a one-hour television special. The seductive Madame Zajj (essentially, the word jazz spelled backwards), was performed by a rising star of dance, Carmen de Lavallade (1931–). She appears in the center of the drum (symbolizing the drum turning into a woman) lip synching to Margaret's voice, seducing the male lead, Joe to convince him to come with her. Ellington appears (in tails, what else?) to narrate, explaining that the drum turned into a woman when Joe touched it and telling how Zajj offered him fame and fortune if only he'd come with her as she went around the world—but he refused to go because he was in love with the jungle. Although we hear her haunting soprano from the beginning, Margaret doesn't appear until the end of Act III, to sing the theme, with Ellington behind her conducting the orchestra. She is in her signature strapless gown with a long scarf draped round her neck and one end of it attached to her right glove, providing dramatic effect.

I had the opportunity to watch *A Drum Is a Woman* at the Museum of Film and Television in New York, which is now the Paley Center for Media. I was thrilled to see it

and, just as happened with the beautiful images I saw in the old *Jet* and *Hue* magazines and vintage issues of newspapers like the *Chicago Defender*, I knew that I wouldn't be the only one. *Vintage Black Glamour* is meant to put black pioneers in various fields—who had been forgotten, tucked away in a library or archive—back in the spotlight.

Vintage Black Glamour is a visual tribute to some of the glamorous, accomplished, and often groundbreaking black women—both legendary and obscure—of the 20th century, from 1900 to 1980. It is hardly exhaustive, but it features many photographs that were either previously unseen or not published in half a century or more. There have been many books about the classic glamour and achievements of Hollywood stars, socialites, and fashion models—but it is rare to find a balanced representation, if any, of black women in that mix. *Vintage Black Glamour* celebrates the glamour and achievements of inspirational women who were not always recognized as such. Even though we know about goddesses like Josephine Baker (1906–1975) and powerhouses like the great Madam C.J. Walker (1867–1919), somehow their peers seem to be invisible, except to a few select scholars and avid fans of black American history.

One of my favorite actresses, the late Rosalind Cash (1938–1995), once said, "There are a lot of us who would like to assimilate all the glamour and fluff, but the hard truth is, we're all out here trying to make a living." I think that many of the women featured in these pages would agree with that assessment. But I also believe that as they put in the hard work, they enjoyed quite a bit of that glamour and fluff. It is that sentiment, along with the inspiration of John H. Johnson's simple edict when he founded *Ebony* magazine in 1945—to "show not only the Negroes but also white people that Negroes got married, had beauty contests, gave parties, ran successful businesses, and did all the other normal things of life"—that drives *Vintage Black Glamour*. The highest form of praise anyone could receive from the great Duke Ellington was that they were "beyond category," and the women in these pages truly do fit that definition. Whether they were triple threat singers, dancers, and actors creating and performing art that defied stereotypes; entertainers reborn as entrepreneurs; or musicians unlimited by genre, "beyond category" only begins to describe these women.

Words can be powerful, but sometimes a photograph is even more so, especially when you consider that many of the subjects in this book faced obstacles that had nothing to do with their talent and that ultimately excluded them from history. If there is a place for cliché here, the expression "a picture is worth a thousand words" has never been more fitting.

Margaret Tynes with Harry Belafonte in Chicago on June 1, 1956. She was the leading lady in Mr. Belafonte's off-Broadway musical, *Sing Man, Sing!*

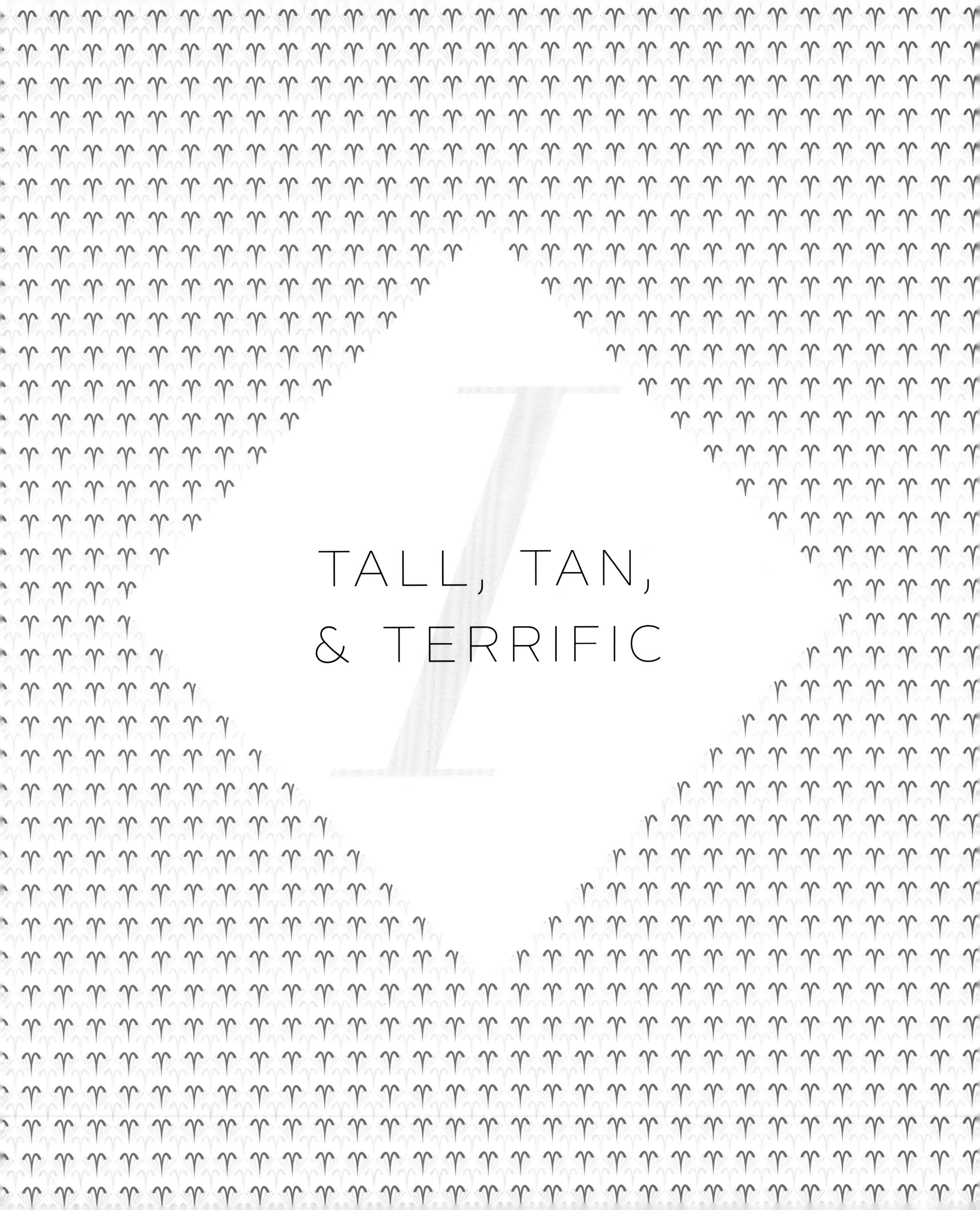

I

TALL, TAN, & TERRIFIC

Selika Lazevski, photographed by Felix Nadar in Marseille, in 1891. It is not known whether she was a horsewoman or an artist's model, but there is no question about her striking beauty.

ON OCTOBER 5, 1892, "the greatest demonstration ever attempted by race women for one of their own number" was held at Lyric Hall in New York City. It was an elegant testimonial, held in honor of the writer of those words, Ida B. Wells, in gratitude for her courageous anti-lynching work in the American South. As Paula Giddings described it in her groundbreaking book, *When and Where I Enter: The Impact of Black Women on Race and Sex in America* (1996), the women in attendance were "a veritable Who's Who of the Black eastern establishment" including Dr. Susan McKinney Steward, the first African-American woman to earn a medical doctorate in New York State and the third in the United States. Josephine St. Pierre Ruffin, a Boston suffragist and publisher of the first black woman's newspaper, *The Women's Era*, was there as well as Victoria Earle Matthews, the journalist and social worker born a slave who founded the White Rose Mission, a home designed to protect and educate young, working African-American women who were new to New York City. Electric lights on the dais beamed "Iola," Wells' pen name, and music and speeches were offered as $500 was collected for her booklet, *Southern Horror: Lynch Law in All Its Phases.*

By 1895, these women gathered again, this time to address the vicious maligning of black women in an article by James W. Jacks, a white Missouri newspaper editor who was also the president of the Missouri Press Association. Citing "evidence" from other black women, Jacks wrote a letter attacking black women for their alleged lack of virtue and sent it to a British anti-lynching society after Ida B. Wells returned from an extremely effective and influential speaking tour where she addressed lynching. Ruffin and the other women swiftly responded by organizing a conference to address Jacks' letter and further pressing social issues that concerned black women. Navigating in such a hostile atmosphere made many black women especially careful about the image of themselves that they projected, particularly when it concerned black female sexuality and how it was perceived publicly. Popular novels of the day by black women authors, largely influenced by Victorian mores and ideas of respectability, depicted noble black women who struggled to defend and preserve the "priceless gem of virginity." There were magazines aimed expressly at "Afro-American" women, the first being *Ringwood's Afro-American Journal of Fashion*, which appeared in 1891 and was published for four years. Later, other magazines, including *Half-Century Magazine for the Colored Home and Homemaker* and *The Sepia Socialite*, would make brief appearances, decades before *Essence* was introduced in May 1970. The gathering of club women in 1895 was one of the earliest examples of black women being concerned about how they were presented in the media. As Deborah Gray White noted in her book, *Too Heavy a Load: Black Women in Defense of Themselves, 1894–1994* (1999), these women knew that they "had to become their own persuasive argument" if they wanted to see the race, and black women in particular, succeed.

During this era, black women were succeeding in many areas where they were not expected to excel. The Whitman Sisters, superstar entertainers, were well aware of the idea of being their "own persuasive argument" and conducted themselves accordingly. The sisters owned and produced their own performing company, which traveled across the United States from the turn of the century until 1940, making them the longest-running and highest-paid act on the African-American–run Theater Owners Booking Association (T.O.B.A.). Ever loyal to the African-American community, the Whitmans entertained whites and blacks, men and women, upper-, middle-, and lower-class Americans. Their biographer, Nadine George-Graves, explains in her book, *The Royalty of Negro Vaudeville: The Whitman Sisters and the Negotiation of Race, Gender and Class in African American Theater 1900–1940*

Aida Overton Walker (1880–1914) in the 1903 London production of *In Dahomey*. At the age of 16, she toured the United States with the Black Patti Troubadours before joining Williams and Walker in 1898.

(2000), that the Whitman sisters "had to carefully control the images they portrayed in order to stay in the 'big time.'" From the time they performed in front of their first audiences, singing and dancing on their father's evangelical tour, through their years as an independent troupe playing the top vaudeville houses of their time as headliners on the T.O.B.A. circuit, to the end of their illustrious 40-year careers, Mabel (1880–1942), Alberta (1887–1963), Essie (1882–1963), and Alice (1900–1969) made sure that they were never taken advantage of, and maintained spotless reputations. Their act thrived before racially mixed audiences who enjoyed the variety of dances, songs, and comedy skits performed for them. In various parts of their act, the sisters wore blackface, cross-dressed, and donned blond wigs to appear like white women. White audiences were often amused—and relieved—to discover that the sisters were African-American. Essie Whitman once said, "The audience was always puzzled and someone was sure to ask, 'What are those white women doing up there?' Then they would recognize us as the performers (they had just seen) and laugh in amazement." Eventually, the sisters decided to play exclusively for black audiences because, as Mabel put it, they felt as if they were "breaking in where we were not really wanted" whereas black audiences gave them "full appreciation without grudge."

Also around this time, Sissieretta Jones gave several successful performances in the north east and certainly did not confuse audiences with her appearance as her career gained momentum. Born Matilda Sissieretta Joyner in Portsmouth, Virginia in 1868 (d. 1933), she was raised in Providence, Rhode Island, where she benefitted from a recent law that abolished segregation in public schools. As a result, she was able to attend with white and black classmates. In 1888 she made her singing debut in New York City and was the first African-American singer to perform at Carnegie Hall. Grudgingly acknowledged as attractive (one reviewer said "she is of full Negro blood, but pleasing to look at"), she sang both operatic and popular songs and toured South America and the Caribbean, where she was gifted diamonds and rubies. She also sang for the Prince of Wales in London and was among the earliest black performers to sing at the White House when she sang for President Benjamin Harrison in 1892. In later years, she formed the successful group, the Black Patti Troubadours. Although she preferred to be known and addressed as Madame Jones, she was given a nickname that would follow her for the rest of her career—"the Black Patti," which compared her to the Spanish-born soprano Adelina Patti.

The seed for her career and others to follow was planted by a few black women singers who came before her. There was Flora Batson Bergen (1864–1906), who lived in Providence just as Jones did. There were also Nellie Brown Mitchell (1845–1924); Marie Selika Williams (1849–1937), who was born in Natchez, Mississippi; and Elizabeth Taylor-Greenfield (1824–1876), born a slave (also in Mississippi) and the best-known black singer of her time, but derided as inelegant and even coarse by some critics. Taylor-Greenfield was largely self-taught because white teachers always turned her down, even when she would offer far more money than they normally would get for lessons. Yet there were music critics of the day who agreed that, with training, Greenfield could have been rather phenomenal.

"I want to be an actor lady"

Ada Overton Walker, born on Valentine's Day, 1880, in New York City to Moses and wardrobe mistress Pauline Whitfield Overton, was raised in a section of Greenwich Village in lower Manhattan that was referred to as "Little Africa" because of the black population that had lived there since the seventeenth century. Overton Walker, who the revered

composer James Weldon Johnson called "the brightest star among women on the Negro stage," was the most popular and highest-paid female entertainer of her era. Late in her career, she changed her name from Ada to Aida, reportedly in homage to the heroine of Verdi's nineteenth-century opera. She began her career in the chorus of Sissieretta Jones' Black Patti Troubadours. Once she joined the comedian and singer Bert Williams and her future husband, George Walker, in their Williams & Walker act, she choreographed all of their routines. One of her most popular dances capitalized on the "Salomania" fad in choreography, which was based on the infamous biblical character usually played by white dancers. In dancing the role, she defied the idea that modern dance was solely the domain of white women. However, mindful of her black audience, she suppressed the expected erotic elements of the dance. Indeed, some reviews of her act would emphasize the modesty of her costume and the "lack of vulgarity, and gracefulness" in her routine. Overton Walker's Rosetta Lightfoot character in the 1902 musical *In Dahomey* "operates as the archetypal voice of black social climbing in the musical," as one reviewer stated. She sang three of the show's most popular numbers: "I Want to Be An Actor Lady" is a "jaunty ragtime number" that expressed Rosetta Lightfoot's ambitions for success and opportunities. A song by James Weldon Johnson and Will Marion Cook called "Leader of the Colored Aristocracy" reaffirms Rosetta's desire to rise to a higher station in life. There was also "Vassar Girl," a song about a "dark belle" who, dressed to the nines, breaks the color barrier and enters the elite college, which was all-white at the time.

In 1908, during the run of the musical *Bandana Land*, her husband became ill and Overton Walker donned his costume and performed his routine along with her own. During the run of the show, Bert Williams made a parody of her Salome dance, which some scholars observe she may have felt compromised her own very serious rendition. By 1912, after the death of her husband the previous year, she was touring the country in a solo show with a revamped version of her Salome dance. Overton Walker also popularized the cakewalk, the nineteenth-century dance craze that originated on slave plantations. Although critics have written that it is likely that she was influenced by Isadora Duncan, who toured America between 1908 and 1911, Overton Walker had transformed herself from vaudeville star to cakewalker, and from actress to modern dancer, before Duncan became famous. Dancing the cakewalk at the end of *In Dahomey* represented to some (as Brooks put it), "a way to conclude and contain the narrative," a showcase of diverse black interests, "with a return to the familiar terrain of the 'happy darkey' plantation motifs often associated with the dance." As Overton Walker famously remarked in an interview with the London *Tatler*, during *In Dahomey*'s British tour in 1902, the dance was meant to convey a seamless and infectious joy for performers and audience alike.

Arguably the leading dancer of her era, Overton Walker urged her colleagues and students who danced the cakewalk to "hold sunshine in [their] hearts. Think of moonlight nights and pine knots and tallow dips, and of lives untouched by the hardness of toil." She would later say, "The success of cakewalking depends on temperament," which invited misinterpretation by a British interviewer who presumed that black dancers should be smiling all of the time because it is characteristic of their race. Daphne Brooks observed in her book, *Bodies in Dissent: Spectacular Performances of Race and Freedom, 1850–1910* (2006):

> We might do well to reconsider the extent of Walker's "Salome" performances in relation to the specific culture and political intent the actress espoused throughout her career. Indeed, as Walker was openly aligned with black uplift and women's era social

and political agendas, it is critical to imagine the performer's lifelong dedication to creating art by and for black people, as her husband had similarly proclaimed in a New York Age article in 1908. In this regard, Walker did not, then, just use "Salome" to "try and transcend her identifications with race comedy." Rather, her work was clearly in dialogue with racial uplift, black nationalist, and black women's culture discourse of the period.

Brooks went on to say that Walker's interpretation of the dance allowed her to absorb and reinvent Salome's legacy of desire, corporeal expression, and rebellious female vision, thus conjoining her potent legend with that of post-bellum New Negro womanhood.

THE UNDENIABLE ELEGANCE of the dance team of Norton and Margot turned out to be a blessing and a curse for their career. Beautiful Harlem-born Marjorie Smith (1910-2005) changed her name to Margot Webb, and she and her dapper friend Harold Norton billed themselves as "Norton and Margot," but their elegant presentation of adagio-style dance limited their career opportunities because it was considered "genteel" and, essentially, "white"—white audiences preferred seeing whites or light-skinned Latinos performing it. As Brenda Dixon Gottschild explained in her book, *Waltzing in the Dark: African American Vaudeville and Race Politics in the Swing Era* (1999), black performers were expected to have rhythm and speed when they danced, and Norton and Margot "were plagued by white audiences urging them to 'get hot' when heat was neither their forte nor appropriate for their genre." Nevertheless, they pressed on for nearly a decade. Norton and Margot opened a dance studio in central Harlem in 1936, but at the height of their performing career, their busy touring schedule meant they were unable to successfully balance the two responsibilities and they had to close the school in 1938. Webb appeared in walk-on parts in low-budget black films in between dance engagements.

Norton and Margot booked their shows by word of mouth because they operated for most of their career without the benefit of a manager. They also shelled out a large portion of their (meager) earnings for photos, wardrobe, and musical arrangements. Webb posed for many promotional glamour shots, including one with nail designs decades before it would be a trend and a lucrative business. She also coached beauty contestants before pageants and chaperoned them at events. She told Dixon Gottschild that dwindling opportunities solidified her decision to return to school. As she balanced family life with her husband and two children and the final days of her dance career, she earned a bachelor's degree at Hunter College in 1940 and a master's degree in education from Columbia University Teachers College in 1948.

While performers like Webb benefitted from the accepted practice of the Cotton Club and other venues of only selecting dancers with the lightest complexions, talents like Lucille Wilson (1914–1983) took exception to that rule. A beautiful, unquestionably gifted, dark-skinned dancer from the Bronx, Wilson auditioned for the Cotton Club in spite of the unwritten color rule. The managers of the club hired her on a trial basis, telling her plainly that they would have to fire her if customers complained. They did not, and she remained at the club for eight years, only quitting her dancing career when she married Louis Armstrong in 1942 and devoted her life to being at his side. It was Lucille who placed a down payment on a home in her old neighborhood, Corona, in the borough of Queens in New York, even

though her husband had no interest in buying a home after decades of hotel living. Queens was home to a slew of black superstars at the time, from Lena Horne to James Brown, and the Armstrongs lived there until their respective deaths in 1971 and 1983. Lucille Armstrong left her entire estate to the Louis Armstrong Educational Foundation, Inc. and their home to the City of New York. The Armstrong home is now the landmarked Louis Armstrong House Museum.

"Hollywood had no parts for me"

Oscar Micheaux, the first African-American to produce a feature-length film, wrote an article in May 1919 called "The Negro and the Photoplay," where he noted, "Before we expect to see ourselves featured on the silver screen as we live, hope, act, and think today, men and women must write original stories of Negro life." He went on to say that "money must be risked in Negro corporations for this purpose." Until that time, most black actors and actresses, aside from those who worked with Micheaux himself, had no other choice but to look for work in white productions. Nina Mae McKinney (1912–1967) was the first black performer to be signed to a long-term contract by a major Hollywood studio in 1929. Her five-year contract with MGM didn't yield much in the way of roles, as it turned out, but that was not apparent at the start, and McKinney's star initially rose. The excitement over her achievement was palpable and she was breathlessly covered by the black press, which was hopeful about seeing the beautiful new movie star succeed in Hollywood. Any excuse was taken to write about her, from legitimate news to non-stories ("Nina to wear Paris creation to party"), and she was more than happy to assist in that regard, sometimes planting stories about her personal life to remain in the spotlight. The *Chicago Defender* sent a photographer to capture Oscar DePriest, the only black in Congress at the time, on a visit to Hollywood to thank King Vidor for producing Nina's star-making vehicle, *Hallelujah*. The photo shows the eighteen-year-old newly minted movie star looking on as Congressman DePriest talks to the famous director. A few weeks later, the *Defender* reported on the Hollywood premiere of the film, noting that, "there was no color line drawn in the enthusiasm with which the star was greeted." In attendance that night were white stars like Charlie Chaplin, Jack Benny, and Norma Shearer with her husband, the director Irving Thalberg. Always with an eye on people of color in high places, the *Defender* reporter opened the story by mentioning the presence of "Kagatjata" Singh, maharajah of Kapurthala, misspelling the first name of Jagatjit Singh, the globe-trotting Hindu prince. The maharajah, according to the paper, "has been the idol of white society in each large city from New York to the west coast," and "registered complete and absolute blank astonishment" over scenes depicting plantation workers in the film.

McKinney was a relative newcomer to New York from her native Lancaster, South Carolina, when she scored a job performing in the chorus of the Broadway show *Blackbirds of 1928*. King Vidor was in the audience one night and immediately cast the chorus girl he remembered as the "third girl from the left" in his film *Hallelujah*, opposite the handsome actor and singer Daniel L. Haynes. Film historian and biographer Donald Bogle wrote in his book *Bright Boulevards, Bold Dreams: The Story of Black Hollywood* (2005) that McKinney lived the glamorous life expected of a Hollywood movie star in the aftermath of what would be the biggest hit of her career. She spent lots of money on clothes, jewelry, and later, drugs. She partied hard with fellow actors, black and white, and even "took up with a maharajah," very likely the aforementioned Singh since there weren't many other

Nina Mae McKinney (1913–1967) in Berlin around 1929. Best known for her starring role in the 1929 film *Hallelujah*, McKinney was born in Lancaster, South Carolina. She found that stardom and a five-year MGM contract still did not bring her roles, so she moved to Europe where she enjoyed great success as a cabaret singer. In the U.K. she starred in two films with Paul Robeson, *Congo* in 1930 and *Sanders of the River* in 1935. She also appeared in *Safe in Hell* in 1931, *Pie, Pie, Blackbird* in 1932, and *Pinky* in 1949.

maharajahs, if any, around at the time. McKinney, glorified as "the dusky Clara Bow" at the beginning of her career, was known as "the Black Garbo" when she sang in cafés in Europe, after solid roles failed to materialize despite that contract with MGM. She had gone to Europe after completing two short films, *Black Network* and *Pie, Pie Blackbird*, the latter starring Eubie Blake, the legendary jazz and ragtime composer and lyricist who co-wrote the pioneering black Broadway musical *Shuffle Along*, and the dancing Nicholas Brothers, who were teenagers at the time. McKinney also starred in *Sanders of the River* in 1935 with Paul Robeson, a film he later disowned because of the imperialist plot edited into the film at the last minute. "I hate the picture," he said a few years after the movie's release. "It is the only film of mine that can be shown in Italy or Germany, for it shows the Negro as Fascist states desire him—savage and childish." McKinney's last memorable film appearance was as the villainous Rozelia in the 1949 film, *Pinky*, a role that shocked and disappointed some fans. As her looks began to fade in the early 1950s, the result of rumored drug and alcohol abuse, she played maids in a few films before dropping out of sight. Her death in 1967 at the age of fifty-four was barely noted in the media, but she was inducted into the Black Filmmakers Hall of Fame in 1978.

Many early black entertainers had at least one first on their resumé. Ethel Waters (1896–1977) had a handful: the first to record and popularize standard songs like "Stormy Weather" and "St. Louis Blues"; the first black actress to star with an all-white cast on Broadway; the first African-American to perform on the radio. She was nominated for an Academy Award in 1949 for her role in *Pinky*, and in 1962 was the first African-American to be nominated for an Emmy Award, for a role in an episode of *Route 66*. Her bleak, poverty-stricken childhood led her to leave home at a very early age. She did domestic work as she began a career singing in clubs. As her popularity grew, she moved on to theater. Waters was known for her razor-sharp wit and once said that Carl Van Vechten, the white photographer and Harlem Renaissance habitué, knew "more about Harlem than any other white man except the captain of the Harlem police station." Unlike other "hot" stars of the day, Waters was not particularly fond of Van Vechten's lavish and infamous parties. "I told Carl the caviar looked like buckshot to me—and didn't taste much better." Presumably Van Vechten enjoyed the meal she would later prepare for him: "ham and mustard greens, lemon meringue pie, and iced tea."

Etta Moten's clothes weren't glamorous in her brief but memorable appearance in Joan Blondell's *Gold Diggers of 1933*, but her role caused a stir in the black community, proud to see a black woman on film dress and comport herself in a dignified manner. The woman whom Lena Horne called a role model caused a sensation in the black press of her day with her (uncredited) rendition of "My Forgotten Man." She sang the Oscar-nominated song "The Carioca" in the very first Fred Astaire and Ginger Rogers film, *Flying Down to Rio* (1933), in character as a Brazilian singer. She also dubbed singing voices for Rogers and Barbara Stanwyck nearly a decade before she made her Broadway debut in the 1935 production of *Porgy and Bess* with the baritone Todd Duncan. All of this came after she earned a bachelor's degree in voice and drama at the age of thirty in 1931 from the University of Kansas, and that after she left a youthful marriage that had led to three children. Sidney Poitier, who made one of his first Broadway appearances with her in *Lysistrata* in 1946, sent a letter to her for her 100th birthday celebration in 2001 in which he called her "the most incredible, amazing, voluptuous, dignified, and sensual actress to grace the Broadway stage in my lifetime." A native of Weimar, Texas who lived the rest of her life in Chicago, Moten would observe late in life, "I didn't know how hard it was to get the parts I auditioned for. Otherwise, I would have been scared to death. That's the story of my life and, I guess, what saved me. I never realized the difficulties I faced until it was all over." She died in 2004.

Theresa Harris (1906–1985) played a series of maids to nearly every major Hollywood star of the time, from Bette Davis and Jean Harlow to Ginger Rogers and Esther Williams. In *Baby Face* (1933) Barbara Stanwyck played Lily Powers, an ambitious gold digger who later questions her ways. Ms. Harris played her best friend and "maid" Chico, who is with her every step of the way as she climbs the ladder of success, one man (or two) at a time. One of the few times she was not typecast as a maid, she played the girlfriend of Eddie "Rochester" Anderson's character in two 1940s films, *Buck Benny Rides Again* and *Love Thy Neighbor*. Donald Bogle described Harris in *Bright Boulevards, Bold Dreams: The Story of Black Hollywood* as "both outspoken and highly intelligent" and noted that she "didn't mince words about the plight of colored actresses." Harris told Fay M. Jackson of the *California Eagle*, an African-American newspaper, in August 1937:

> I never felt the chance to rise above the role of maid in Hollywood movies. My color was against me. The fact that I was not "hot" stamped me as either an uppity "Negress" or relegated me to the eternal role of stooge or servant. I can sing but so can hundreds of other girls. My ambitions are to be an actress. Hollywood had no parts for me.

Ms. Harris would later tell the same reporter that she enjoyed working in race movies "because in the picture I have the chance of wearing clothes." "Clothes," as in a gorgeous wardrobe that black women usually never had a chance to wear in white movies. Ms. Harris was the inspiration behind Lynn Nottage's acclaimed 2011 play, *By the Way, Meet Vera Stark*.

Fredi Washington (1903–1994) is mostly remembered for her steadfast refusal to pass as white to advance her film career, but she also spent a great deal of time working to improve conditions for black people on and off the screen. Born Fredricka Carolyn Washington in Savannah, Georgia, she began her career a chorus girl in the first hit black Broadway musical, *Shuffle Along*, in 1921 and toured Europe as a dancer with partner Al Moiret. Appearances in films like *Black and Tan* with Duke Ellington in 1929 and *The Emperor Jones* with Paul Robeson in 1933 made her a household name in black homes. Washington was well acquainted with Ellington through her marriage to Lawrence Brown, a trombonist in his orchestra. She often traveled with them in the southern part of the United States, passing as white to buy food in whites-only restaurants for the band. A bold, plain-spoken civil rights activist who was once photographed wearing over a smart suit and a simple but powerful armband that depicted a lynched man, she turned her frustration about limited acting opportunities into action by co-founding the Negro Actors Guild of America in 1936. She counted Duke Ellington, Ethel Waters, and Paul Robeson among members of the board. "There were months and years in between parts," she would later say. "And it's hard to build and polish a craft that way." The goal of the Negro Actors Guild was to challenge the entertainment industry to change persistent stereotypical images of black people in film and on the stage. Washington was also the drama editor and theater critic for *The People's Voice*, a weekly newspaper in New York that was published by Adam Clayton Powell, Jr., a charismatic Harlem politician and minister who was married to her sister Isabel at the time. Washington wrote two regular columns for the paper, "Headlines and Footlights" and "Fredi Speaks." After her second marriage in 1951, to Dr. Hugh Anthony Bell, Washington spent the rest of her days in Connecticut, where she died at the age of 90 after a bout of pneumonia.

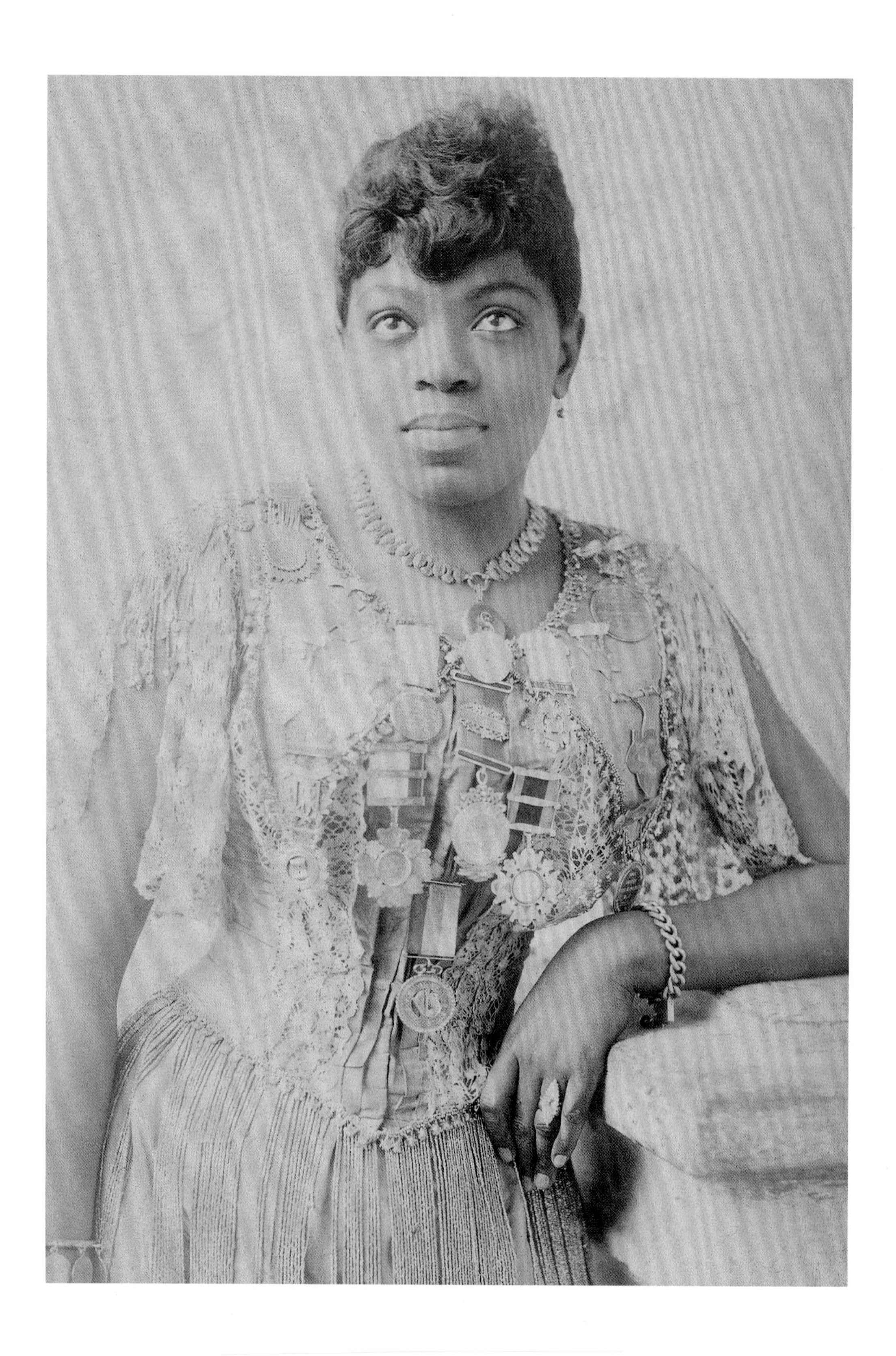

1/1

MATILDA SISSIERETTA JONES

Seen here in 1889, she preferred to be called Madame Jones (1868/69–1933) but was better known as "the Black Patti," which compared her to the Italian soprano Adelina Patti. She made her professional debut in New York City in 1888, and was the first African-American singer to perform at Carnegie Hall. She also performed with Fisk University's popular Jubilee Singers and toured the world, especially Europe and South America. She sang for President Benjamin Harrison at the White House in 1892.

1/2

SAIDIE SELLYNA

An actress, singer, and dancer, seen here in a publicity photo circa 1911. She worked as a singer and dancer in Russia in the 1920s; little else is known about her.

1/3
FLORENCE MILLS

One of the earliest black superstars, Florence Mills (1895–1927), seen here in *Dover Street to Dixie* at the London Pavilion in 1923, was best known as the lead in the first all-black Broadway musical, *Shuffle Along*, in 1921. Her sudden death in 1927 at the height of her popularity devastated friends and fans in the United States and Europe. An estimated 150,000 people lined the streets of Harlem to mourn her passing.

1/4

ADELAIDE HALL

She began her career as a chorus member in *Shuffle Along* in 1921, was the star of *Chocolate Kiddies* in 1925, and became the first black star to be given a long-term contract with the BBC. Hall (1901–1993), photographed here in *Blackbirds of 1928*, had her own radio series in the U.K. and lived there for over 40 years. Her last performance was at Carnegie Hall on her 90th birthday.

1/5

JOSEPHINE BAKER

In one of the pictures from her 1951 comeback performance in New York, Josephine Baker, three months shy of her 45th birthday, looks stunning. Clad in Dior, she is curvaceous with a bit of belly and unapologetically self-possessed. This image was a stark contrast from the eager, smiling, nubile dancer who mesmerized French audiences with her infamous *danse sauvage* some twenty-five years earlier. As a 19-year-old newcomer to Paris in 1925, the brightly colored homemade outfits the St. Louis-born Josephine wore made quite the unintended impression, as she later explained. "My attire made everyone laugh. Now, I'll tell you why everyone laughed and I laugh about it more than anyone else. I wore a checkered dress with pockets held up by two checkered suspenders over my checkered blouse. I wore a hat with feathers on the top of my head, and I carried a camera on my left hip, and a large pair of binoculars on my right hip."

As a rising star in Paris, she "locked horns" with Paul Poiret, the French designer credited with doing away with petticoats and the first designer to create a brand that extended beyond fashion ("He said blue, I said pink"). It was Poiret who draped her in the famous gown that would become known as the *robe Josephine* and inspired her signature sleek, short hairstyle—something she may not have foreseen during her first visit with him.

She later said of the meeting, "I was quickly stripped of my clothes by two young women who instinctively sensed their master's wishes. Here I was, nude again. At least I was getting used to it. A third flunky now appeared, carrying a bolt of the most beautiful silvery material I had ever seen. It looked like a flowing river. Monsieur Poiret poured the gleaming torrent over me, rolled me up in it, draped it about my body, pulled it tight, ordered me to walk, and then loosened it around my legs. I felt like a sea goddess emerging from the foam."

She opened her own cabaret called Chez Josephine and it swiftly became home to a number of black American expatriate musicians and artists in the 1920s and 1930s. Biographer Bennetta Jules-Rosette wrote (in *Josephine Baker In Art And Life*) that she both benefited and suffered from her complicity in the primal image that would forever shadow her career, beginning with her famous banana skirt.

"I *had* to succeed," Josephine explained, "I would never stop trying, never. A violinist had his violin, a painter his palette. All I had was myself. I was the instrument that I must care for, just as Sidney [Bechet] fussed over his clarinet. That's why I spent thirty minutes every morning rubbing my body with half a lemon to lighten my skin and just as long preparing a mixture for my hair. I couldn't afford to take chances."

1/6

JOSEPHINE BAKER

Wearing a modest cut-out dress, posing in classical surroundings of her beloved Château des Milandes, in the Dordogne, France, her home from 1937 to 1969.

1/7

JOSEPHINE BAKER

Taking an after-show cocktail in Venice, Italy, 1940.

1/8

PRINCESS KOUKA OF SUDAN

"I don't care if she doesn't speak English. I don't care if she's had no experience. She's got what it takes." So said English producer Walter Futter, who hand-picked Princess Kouka (1915–?) for the role of Gara in the 1937 film *Jericho*, in which she starred with Paul Robeson, and for which this photo was taken. The princess, daughter of Sheik Ibrahim Mahdi, spoke French and no English and "spent three days prettying up in Paris" before arriving in London to complete her role in the film. Dressed in a "gold lace veil, royal blue jacket embroidered with silver wire, scarlet silk skirt, six-inch earrings of beaten gold, a gold filigree girdle and bracelets inset with coral and turquoise," the Princess had a press day at London's Claridge's Hotel and was interviewed by multiple reporters with the aid of an interpreter. She said her father was "horrified" when Futter asked her to be in the film and would not grant permission. She cried, locked herself in her room and refused to eat. He finally relented, saying if she was "going to die of hunger anyway, she might just as well do as revolting a thing as act in films."

1/9

CHORUS GIRLS

Photographed at the Apollo Theater in Harlem, in 1936, by Lucien Aigner.

1/10

JENI LEGON

This studio photo from May 1935 shows the Chicagoan dancer (1916–2012), who began her career age just 16 in a chorus line backed by Count Basie's Orchestra. She is probably best remembered for dancing with Bill "Bojangles" Robinson in *Hooray for Love* (1935), which also featured Fats Waller. Incredibly, LeGon was the only black woman to dance with Robinson on screen. She appeared in over 24 films during the course of her career, including *Bright Road* with Dorothy Dandridge and Harry Belafonte in 1953, and *Bones* with Snoop Dogg in 2001.

1/11

FREDI WASHINGTON

The uncompromising actor and civil rights activist (1903–1994) with anti-lynching armband, 1940s.

1/12

IVIE ANDERSON

The California-born singer (1905–1949) performing with Duke Ellington circa 1935. She began in the chorus of *Shuffle Along*, spent a decade touring the world as a soloist, and joined Ellington in 1931.

1/13

MARGOT WEBB

The groundbreaking dancer (1910–2005) in feathers, 1934.

1/14

MARGOT WEBB

Performing her jazzy toe solo in 1941 at the Apollo Theater in New York.

1/15

MARGOT WEBB

With her dance partner, Harold Norton, at the Apollo in 1941.

1/16

BLANCHE DUNN

"... and that stunning colored girl—you know, the one who always goes to first nights." Blanche Dunn (1911–?), a chic Harlem Renaissance–era actress, was essentially an 'It' girl of the era. Photographed by Carl Van Vechten in 1941, whose legendary parties were, as Langston Hughes put it, "so Negro that they were reported as a matter of course in the colored society columns, just as though they occurred in Harlem instead of West 55th street." Richard Bruce Nugent, a wry Harlem Renaissance writer and painter, noted that Dunn was "one of the best-dressed women in New York City" and "at all the Broadway first nights." According to Nugent, Dunn did not come across her sense of style without a bit of help. He credited Cleveland-born dress designer Wilda Gunn for taking the "wide-eyed little girl fresh from the West Indies" under her wing and teaching her the art of dressing well. "A party was not a party, a place not a place, without Blanche."

1/17

ETTA MOTEN

Lena Horne's role model, seen here in a 1934 photo by Carl Van Vechten. A native of Weimar, Texas, Moten (1901–2004) lived the rest of her life in Chicago. She would observe late in life, that "I didn't know how hard it was to get the parts I auditioned for. Otherwise, I would have been scared to death. That's the story of my life and, I guess, what saved me. I never realized the difficulties I faced until it was all over."

SEPIA DREAMGIRLS, PIN-UPS, & HOLLYWOOD STARLETS

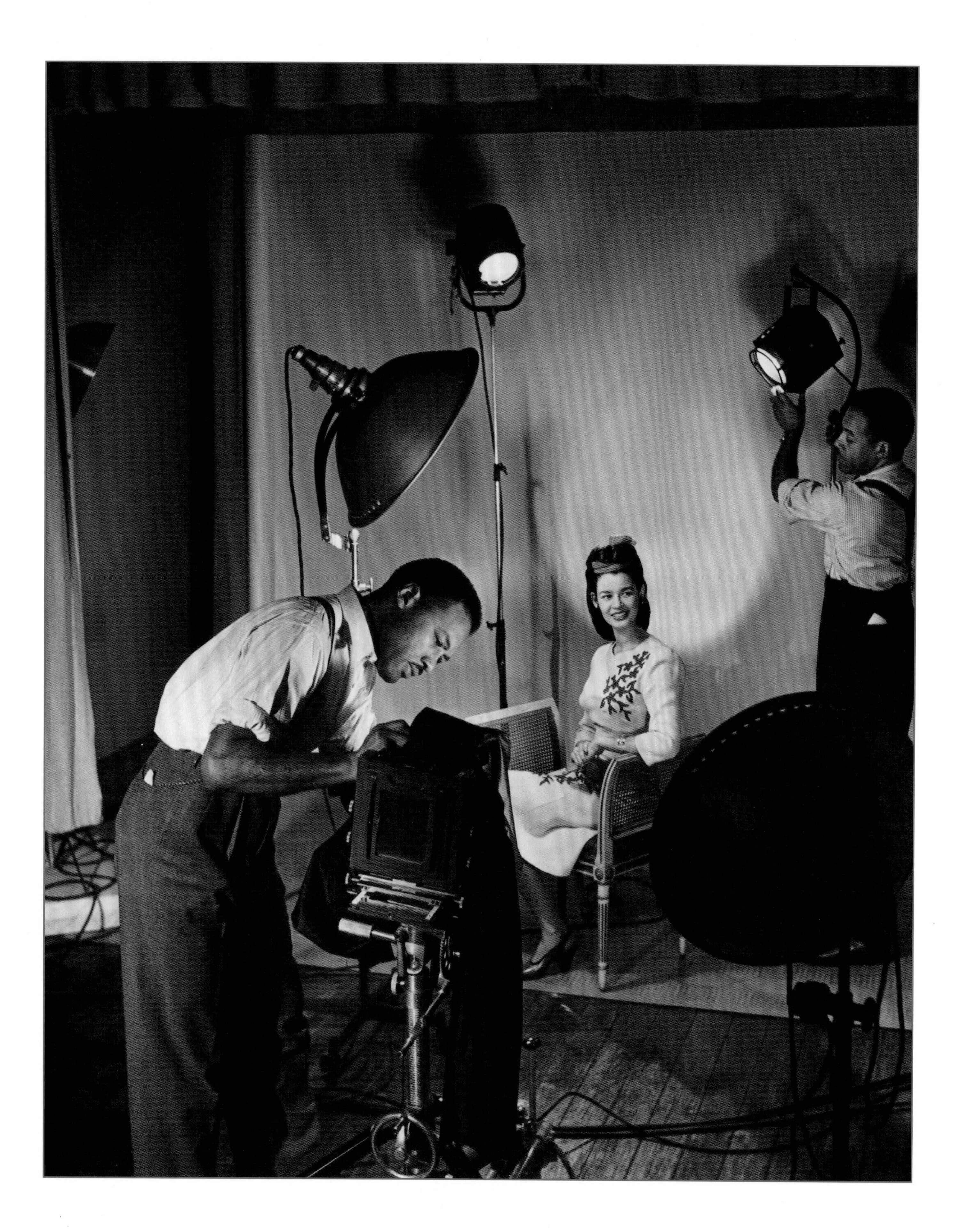

As the distribution and influence of black newspapers and magazines grew, so did the exposure of models, both "big-time" and bold amateurs. It was an environment ripe for scams, and pretty soon articles started to appear in newspapers warning impressionable young women about the pitfalls of pursuing a fleeting career in modeling. In one 1952 article that ran in the *New Jersey Afro-American*, the headline was practically a sneer: *Girls Find Modeling Glamorous, Much Sought After, But Hardly Gainful.* The writer quotes at length one of the top black models at the time, Sara Lou Harris (b. 1926), known to readers for appearing in ads for Lucky Strike cigarettes, a feat which made her the first black model to appear in a national print advertisement. Harris, a former cashier at the Savoy Ballroom in Harlem and 1943 graduate of Bennett College, a historically black college for women, in Greensboro, South Carolina, said, "While the modeling field is gradually opening up to Negro women, it still hasn't reached the place where we colored women can depend solely on modeling for a livelihood. Actually, there are only one or two Negro models whose earnings are high enough to afford a comfortable living from modeling alone. For all other Negro models, it is necessary to have a regular job and just use modeling as a sideline." She continued, "To become successful, a girl must also have certain attributes. A quick alert mind is generally considered a prime asset. An important thing to remember is that beautiful girls do not always make the best models. Because of their beauty, they are often a little too much aware of themselves and they fail to have the warmth and love for people that is so necessary in this field. It is important to remember that being yourself is by far your best bet if you want to get ahead in modeling."

Sara Lou Harris, (b. 1926) one of the first black models to appear in advertisements, with twin brother photographers Morgan and Marvin Smith at the Smith studio in Manhattan in 1942.

Although Sara Lou Harris advised aspiring models to be themselves if they wanted to have a chance at making modeling a career, it didn't hurt if you had ingenuity and drive of Dorothea Towles (1922–2006). A graduate of Wiley College in Marshall, Texas, Towles moved to Los Angeles to earn a master's degree in education from the University of Southern California, but soon became restless and on the lookout for a suitable outlet for her creativity and interests. "I wanted to do something like Mary Church Terrell or Mary McLeod Bethune, but I didn't know how," she told Barbara Summers for her book, *Black and Beautiful: How Women of Color Changed the Fashion Industry* (2001). "I didn't have their kind of skills, but I grew up reading about them and knowing about them. I knew about Josephine Baker, too, but to me she was like a myth. So I used to think, 'What can I do?' This was the late '40s." Towles' older sister, Lois, whom she "worshipped," was a classical pianist and music professor at Fisk University. In 1949 Lois Towles took a leave of absence from her professorship to study under famed pianists Nadia Boulanger and Robert Casadesus at their American Conservatory at Fontainebleau near Paris, and Dorothea, unhappy in her marriage to a dentist who was "old enough to be my father," decided to follow her there. "When I got into fashion and saw that I liked it, I wanted to go to the center of the fashion world." After starting out at Christian Dior as a substitute model while one of Dior's regular models was on vacation, Dorothea eventually became a house model. Once the regular model returned, Dior sent her to Madame Schiaparelli and, as Dorothea relayed to Summers, "I worked for her for about a year until I learned the ropes and could get in the swing of what was going down." Towles would have remained in Los Angeles, but coolly observed that "there was nothing going on" for blacks in Hollywood. Towles' prediction about Hollywood didn't seem to be too far off. A 1952 *Jet* magazine article focused on a set of film starlets who struggled in Hollywood, and, in some cases, had already given up on it.

In the 1940s, the fashion industry had to be creative within the limits of wartime regulations. Because fabric had to be preserved at all costs, the emphasis was firmly on accessories, and hats were big. Under these beautiful hats, black women wore bangs, falls, and pompadours, often with the aid of lye-based hair straighteners. Hair straighteners and bleaching creams have long been a bone of contention in the black community and in the early days they represented something of a catch-22. While black newspapers constantly promoted "race pride," right alongside those editorials would be advertisements inviting the reader to get "lighter, brighter, lovelier skin." Marcus Garvey refused to accept advertisements for skin lighteners or hair straighteners for his organization's weekly newspaper, *The Negro World*, in the 1920s, but most black papers at the time did as a matter of survival. Local fashion shows around the country were intimate affairs. The shows usually featured dresses and hats by local designers, and models whom audience members knew from their neighborhood, school, or church. Admission was often free, but guests paid for drinks and sometimes brought their own food.

The "Double v" campaign was started in 1942, just as World War II began for the United States, by the *Pittsburgh Courier*, a historic African-American newspaper. "Double v" stood for "Victory Abroad and Victory at Home" and the purpose was to call continued attention to the legal injustices and segregation that Blacks dealt with as American citizens on American soil and as soldiers abroad within the (segregated) armed forces. To appreciate the role of the *Pittsburgh Courier* in this campaign, bear in mind that white newspapers did not cover blacks unless there was a crime involved or, of course, if the person in question was an athlete or an entertainer. White newspapers did not cover our births, deaths, weddings or any other slice-of-life type of activity that we took part in just like everyone else. That is why, in part, *Ebony* magazine was born. And the white papers certainly did not report on racial discrimination (especially within the military, where black newspapers were banned from libraries during the Double v Campaign) the way the black press did. The "Double v" campaign also provided inspiration for clothing and hairstyles at the time. Men and women wore "Double v" accessories like lapel pins and women flocked to beauty salons to have their hair styled into bold chignons to resemble the letter "V."

Helen Williams (b. 1937) was easily the most consistently working black model of the 1950s and 1960s. The New Jersey native began modeling in 1954 after being encouraged to give it a shot by several black big-name entertainers who passed through her job at Pagano Studios, one of the largest commercial photography houses in Manhattan. Williams was initially employed as an artist but soon learned about styling models before she was convinced to become a model herself. After signing with Ophelia DeVore, she eventually became the most familiar and photographed black model of the era and her solid, steady career opened more doors than she could ever imagine. As Barbara Summers aptly put it, "If there was resistance to pictures of black models *washing* everyday clothes, we can only imagine the depth of resistance to photographs showing black women *wearing* beautiful clothes."

While Towles' observation that "there was nothing going on in Hollywood for blacks" was mostly true, a few black actresses quietly made some headway. Mildred Joanne Smith (1923–) made her only film appearance as Sidney Poitier's wife in *No Way Out* in 1950. However, she was featured in a number of Broadway shows including the abbreviated run of *Lysistrata* in 1946, which starred Etta Moten and included Poitier in a small role. She also appeared in the Duke Ellington musical *Beggar's Holiday* (1948), whose colorblind casting policy led to picketers protesting the performance nearly every night for its brief 114-show run. Under the uncharitable headline "The Magnificent Failure," Smith was the cover subject for the February 28, 1952 issue of *Jet* in a story that followed her as she recovered from a near-fatal plane crash. The article detailed the quality of her leading men (Poitier and the venerable Canada Lee) and the "vagaries" of her career, which included well-reviewed turns on Broadway and in London nightclubs. It was a very short-sighted take on a very respectable career.

Olga James was born in 1930 in Washington, D.C. Her father was a saxophonist and her mother was a dancer on the Chitlin' Circuit. Raised by her grandparents, she attended Juilliard and shared a studio with a future icon, Leontyne Price, as she lived across the river in Newark, New Jersey and worked her way through school. One of her summer jobs was in a New Jersey factory assembling the filaments for light bulbs. She preferred singing German lieder, French chansons, and Mozart songs because she didn't think she had the right voice for opera. An early performing job lead to the film that would make her recognizable to generations. She sang with Larry Steele's Smart Affairs at Club Harlem in Atlantic City. When the revue went to Chicago, a woman who auditioned all Juilliard students remembered Olga and sent her to audition for a new film called *Carmen Jones*, a black version of Georges Bizet's opera, *Carmen*. In 1956, she played the ingénue role of Ethel Pearson on Broadway with Sammy Davis, Jr. in *Mr. Wonderful* and appeared on the cover of *Ebony* with him and Puerto Rican dance legend Chita Rivera. She met her husband, bop saxophonist Julian "Cannonball" Adderley, in 1956 through her friend Frances Taylor Davis, a former Katherine Dunham dancer who appeared with her on Broadway in *Mr. Wonderful* and who was married to Miles Davis at the time. However, Olga and Adderley didn't see each other again until 1960, when they crossed paths at the Mocambo in Los Angeles after her return from the London run of Lorraine Hansberry's *A Raisin in the Sun*. They married two years later. In the 1970s she appeared on *The Bill Cosby Show* as Verna, the sister-in-law of Bill Cosby's Chet Kincaid, and retired from show business soon thereafter.

II/1

LENA HORNE

Looking good was a major part of Lena Horne's career, but she couldn't help but resent the reason why. "I was unique in that I was the kind of black that white people could accept," she once said. "I was their daydream. I had the worst kind of acceptance because it was never for how great I was or what I contributed. It was because of the way I looked." James Gavin noted in his Horne biography, *Stormy Weather: The Life of Lena Horne* (2009), "Other women borrowed from Horne freely, as though her innovations had entered the public domain" and Horne (1917–2010) was not amused. Her position, she felt, informed the professional decisions she made. She turned down a role in the 1946 Broadway musical *St. Louis Woman*, for instance—even though it was written by Harlem Renaissance luminaries Arna Bontemps and Countee Cullen with her in mind—because the National Association for the Advancement of Colored People (NAACP), led by Walter White, felt that the role was a "disgrace to Negro womanhood."

Her battles at MGM Studios were legendary. As only the second black woman to sign a long-term contract with a major movie studio, Horne found that roles were still hard to come by. And getting her hair done was almost as hard. In the book *The Hornes: An American Family* (1986), Horne's daughter, Gail Buckley, explained that the studio's celebrated heads of hairdresing and makeup, Sydney Guilaroff and Jack Dawn, had to attend to her mother because their staff refused to. Buckley also wrote about Horne's love for beautiful and fashionable things, from "Chen-yu lipsticks and Guerlain perfumes" to "prescription pill bottles from MGM's Dr. Feel-good, and books by Agatha Christie, Edna Ferber, Pearl Buck, and John O'Hara." She was also a good friend of Ginette Spanier, the director of the House of Balmain. "Lena poured herself into Balmain's beads, Madame Grès's jerseys, Jean Dessés's chiffons, and Maggy Rouff's hats—at celebrity prices," Buckley wrote. Horne also had a special place in her heart for the department store Bergdorf Goodman, which began with her opening night at the Savoy-Plaza Hotel in 1942. Because MGM was late in sending her dresses for her opening night performance, Lena and her friend Zulme "Nuffie" MacNeal (1915–2008), best known as Cab Calloway's wife of more than fifty years, decided to go shopping at Bergdorf's, across the street from the Savoy-Plaza. MacNeal, a black woman who looked white, held a master's degree in sociology from Howard University and was a researcher for the Nobel Prize–winning Swedish economist Gunnar Myrdal's groundbreaking black American study, *An American Dilemma*, a study that was critical in the dismantling of "separate but equal" laws in the United States. MacNeal and Horne found a gorgeous red lace dress that would have been perfect for the show. But it was early in her career, and she didn't have enough money to buy the dress. The clerk fetched Andrew Goodman, the owner of the store. "Why don't you take the lace dress?" he suggested, adding, "Charge it, and pay for it a little bit at a time."

Although it annoyed Horne when people could not see past her good looks, she did not take them for granted. She exercised every morning, got eight hours of sleep each night, and cut back any drinking when she had to work. Looking back at the age of 80, Horne said: "My identity is very clear to me now. I am a black woman. I'm free. I no longer have to be a 'credit.' I don't have to be a symbol to anybody; I don't have to be a first to anybody. I don't have to be an imitation of a white woman that Hollywood sort of hoped I'd become. I'm me, and I'm like nobody else."

11/2

LENA HORNE

Lena Horne sits for a portrait with Geoffrey Holder in 1959. Best known as a dancer, Holder is also a Tony Award–winning director and costume designer.

11/3

LENA HORNE

Seated, with husband Lennie Hayton, at a Balmain fashion show in Paris, 1957.

11/4

DOROTHEA TOWLES

The model (1922–2006) photographed in Paris, circa 1950, by Morgan and Marvin Smith. The twin brothers often claimed that they weren't always sure which one of them snapped certain photos, and insisted that their work always be credited to both of them.

11/5

THERESA HARRIS

The Houston-born actor (1906–1985) told a reporter for the African-American newspaper *California Eagle* in 1937, "I never felt the chance to rise above the role of maid in Hollywood movies. My color was against me. The fact that I was not 'hot' stamped me as either an uppity Negress or relegated me to the eternal role of stooge or servant. I can sing but so can hundreds of other girls. My ambitions are to be an actress. Hollywood had no parts for me." She was a bit more hopeful in 1952 when she told *Jet* magazine, "All I can do is keep on plugging and hoping."

11/6

JUDY PACE

Seen here working as an Ebony Fashion Fair model, before she made her way to Hollywood. Dubbed "The Thinking Man's Star" by *Ebony* in 1971, Pace (b. 1942) had a recurring role in the seminal 1960s television show Peyton Place and appeared in popular films like *Cotton Comes to Harlem*.

11/7

ABBEY LINCOLN

Born Annie Mae Woolridge, the tenth of twelve children, in Chicago, Abbey Lincoln (1930–2010) had a brief career as a model before her acting and singing career took off. “I sang a song once, in a Jayne Mansfield movie,” Ms. Lincoln told Roger Ebert in 1968. “Then there was nothing else until *Nothing but a Man* in 1965.”

II/8

JOSEPHINE PREMICE

"*. . . a naturally elegant woman who had exquisite taste in everything in life.*" Diahann Carroll on her best friend of more than forty years, the Brooklyn-born Haitian-American Josephine Premice (1926–2001), seen here backstage in 1951. Carroll called Premice "my mentor from the beginning," and credited her with giving fashion advice that "I took with me the rest of my life." A two-time Tony Award nominee, for *Jamaica* in 1958 and the Negro Ensemble Company production *A Hand is on the Gate* in 1967, Premice would go on to star in the popular 1970s Broadway musical *Bubblin' Brown Sugar*.

11/9

JANE WHITE

"In 1945, I was a leading lady on Broadway." Actress Jane White (1922–2011) in a 1941 photograph by Carl Van Vechten. A 1944 graduate of Smith College, she was the daughter of civil rights icon Walter White. She began her career on Broadway in 1945 when Paul Robeson helped her get her first role as the lead in Lillian Smith's *Strange Fruit*, a story about a doomed interracial love affair. Eleanor Roosevelt praised Ms. White's work for its "restraint and beauty." In 1959, she originated the role of Queen Aggravain (to a young Carol Burnett's princess) in *Once Upon a Mattress*. For the role, Ms. White was asked to lighten her complexion, lest she "confuse" the audience with her "Mediterranean" looks. She would go on to establish a solid reputation as an actress in Shakespearean and classical roles from the 1960s through the 1990s. In 1979, her autobiographical one-woman show, *Jane White, Who?...*, was well received, and she worked as a cabaret singer and in film and television, including a small part in the film *Beloved* (1998).

11/10

RUBY DEE

Photo by Carl Van Vechten on September 25, 1964. Born Ruby Ann Wallace (1922–2014) in Cleveland, Ohio, Dee was raised in Harlem, where her schoolteacher mother introduced her to the arts. She attended Hunter College and joined the American Negro Theater, where actors like Sidney Poitier and Harry Belafonte started. In 1950 Dee starred in *The Jackie Robinson Story* as the baseball legend's wife, opposite Robinson himself. In 1958, she appeared in *St. Louis Blues* with an all-star cast that included Eartha Kitt, Ella Fitzgerald, and Mahalia Jackson, and the next year appeared with Diana Sands in Lorraine Hansberry's landmark play *A Raisin in the Sun*. She also partnered her husband Ossie Davis in projects he directed such as *Purlie Victorious* on Broadway, *The Ossie Davis and Ruby Dee Story Hour* on radio, and *With Ossie and Ruby!* on PBS.

11/11

HILDA SIMMS

Photo circa 1940, taking a moment for herself in her dressing room. The groundbreaking Minnesota-born actress (1918–1994) was best known for her starring role in the first all-black production of *Anna Lucasta* on Broadway in 1944. Despite the tremendous momentum provided by the publicity behind the show, she only made two more appearances on Broadway (*The Cool World* in 1960 and *Tambourines to Glory* in 1963) and two films, *The Joe Louis Story* in 1953 and *The Black Widow* in 1954.

11/12

DOROTHY DANDRIDGE

Her transformation from ingénue to glamour icon began with a few tips from Herb Jeffries, the actor best known for recording the song "Flamingo" with Duke Ellington and starring in early black western films. Jeffries met Dandridge when they both appeared in Ellington's 1941 musical *Jump for Joy*. Jeffries had a knack for makeup application and he showed Dandridge how to use it. A professional since the age of seven, Dandridge (1922–1965) essentially grew up on the road, traveling with her actress mother, Ruby Dandridge, and her sister, Vivian Dandridge, from gig to gig as a part of the Wonder Girls. She told *Ebony* in a 1962 cover story, "I heard Elsa Lanchester [the British actress best known for her iconic portrayal of *The Bride of Frankenstein*] say 'An actor must be indestructible.' She was right. Mother was right. That the show must go on is one of life's great philosophies." Dandridge studied at the Actors' Lab, the famous integrated acting school located behind Schwab's Drugstore in Hollywood that was accused of being a communist front because it welcomed people of color. Joseph Papp, the director and producer who founded the Public Theater in New York, was an administrator there at the time, studying directing, and Dandridge's classmates included Marilyn Monroe. Her first major film role was *Bright Road*, a 1953 film based on a short story called "See How They Run," by a black former schoolteacher named Mary Elizabeth Vroman.

For obvious reasons, Dandridge resented the constraints that Hollywood placed on her as an actress. "I could play the part of an Egyptian or an Indian or a Mexican, and I'm certainly not the only one. There are other actors and actresses who can do the same thing. There is no reason why a Negro just has to play a Negro because he's a Negro. White people don't do it. They've even played Negroes."

One afternoon in 1963, she met the Armenian-born director Rouben Mamoulian for lunch at Romanoff's in Los Angeles after he was picked to direct the upcoming film *Cleopatra*. Mamoulian told her that he thought she would be perfect for the starring role. She was frank. "You won't have the guts to go through with this. They are going to talk you out of it." The role went to Elizabeth Taylor.

In an effort to avoid such scenarios, Dandridge made many attempts at creating opportunities for herself. She once joined forces with Nat "King" Cole to pitch ideas to networks about doing a television sitcom together. Cole's famously short-lived television show, *The Nat "King" Cole Show*, was known for its high ratings, high-profile guests, and lack of sponsorship from advertisers who refused to financially back a show hosted by an elegant black man. When he learned that a representative of Max Factor cosmetics had stated that a Negro couldn't sell lipstick for them, Cole retorted, "What do they think we use? Chalk? Congo paint?"

Dandridge described the first idea as a show about "this small-time pair of married performers and all of the things that happen as they climb to success." The second idea would have Cole playing himself and Dandridge playing his starstruck secretary. They were turned down all over town.

Offstage, she tried to uphold the image of the dutiful homemaker when she was married to Harold Nicholas, keeping a spotless house and cooking delicious meals including soul fool—an indulgence she would only allow herself once a week. She was very anxious about her weight, and driven by her desire not to become "heavy and matronly" like her mother, she exercised daily for the rest of her life.

"She really loved dignity and elegance. Almost to a fault," Vivian Dandridge once said about her sister. "This is the thing that she abhorred about the nightclub scene... that she had to get up there and just be strictly a sex symbol." She didn't enjoy nightclubs, but appearing there paid the bills and she worked hard at it, even though it annoyed her.

She once told her best friend, Geri Branton: "Ella Fitzgerald is one of the most talented people in the world, and it embarrasses me that she cannot work the rooms that I work. The reason for it is so horrible. She's not sexy. The men in the audience don't want to take her home and go to bed. And yet she's up there singing her heart out for one-third of the money they're paying me. And I resent being in that category."

As Ms. Branton said, "I liked Dottie for saying those things."

11/13

DOROTHY DANDRIDGE

In Cannes, France on May 13, 1955 posing before a silhouette of herself on a poster for her 1954 film *Carmen Jones*.

11/14

DOROTHY DANDRIDGE

Seen here working with Russian-born dance instructor Olga Lunick in the 1950s.

WIVES & SOCIALITES

JESSIE WILLIAMS DEPRIEST (1870–1961) made national headlines in 1929 when she accepted an invitation from the first lady of the United States, Lou Henry Hoover, to attend a tea at the White House in honor of congressional spouses. Her husband, Oscar DePriest, a Republican congressman from Illinois, was the first African-American elected to Congress in the 20th century and the only black in Congress at the time. Hoover decided to host five teas over a three-week period instead of the customary one or two in an attempt to make DePriest's inclusion smoother and to ruffle as few political feathers as possible. Even though each congressional wife had been screened on her racial views (to decide who would attend which tea), there was still controversy. Although the Hoovers did not publicize the event, word got out and objections came in from across the nation. *TIME* magazine would later simply describe DePriest as a "slender, middle-aged invited guest wearing an afternoon dress of Capri blue chiffon, a grey coat trimmed in moleskin, a small grey hat, moonlight grey hose, [and] snakeskin slippers." Other mainstream newspapers were not as subtle. Incredibly, several southern state legislatures actually passed resolutions condemning Hoover for inviting DePriest. She was also criticized in letters that poured in for bringing "disgrace" to the White House and "damaging her husband's political standing and setting back race relations." For the tea that DePriest actually attended, Hoover had to include her sister, secretaries, and wives of the attorney general and secretary of war, along with a few congressional wives who had already attended previous teas. Hoover strategically arranged for DePriest's invitation to be issued at the last minute, on June 5, for the last tea party, which was scheduled specifically to prevent any boycotts. As Nancy Beck Young noted in her book *Lou Hoover: Activist First Lady* (2004), "Racist-minded congressional spouses would have looked silly had they boycotted the earlier teas to protest an event that had not yet occurred, so they had no choice but to attend."

Jessie Williams DePriest, wife of Congressman Oscar DePriest, photographed by Addison Scurlock in 1929 on the day she attended a congressional wives' tea at the White House.

DePriest, undoubtedly cognizant of the importance of the occasion, was photographed that day by one of the premiere black photographers of the day, Addison Scurlock, founder of the Scurlock Photographic Studio. Sara Pelham Speaks, a reporter from a prominent black newspaper family, was very detailed in her breathless account of DePriest's appearance at the tea, writing that she "wore a charming afternoon ensemble of the loveliest pale blue georgette. The simplicity of the costume was only relieved by a beautiful rhinestone buckle, on the left side of the finely pleated skirt. A coat, the shortest of jackets, completed the costume. She wore a large hat of rosy-gray hair braid, trimmed with a cluster of hand-cut dove-gray velvet leaves, and a velvet rose placed modishly on the underbrim, framed her face becomingly. She carried a lovely bag which matched her hat, rosy-gray watersnake slippers, and a large pointed fox scarf." DePriest was escorted through the main entrance to the Green Room by White House staff who were more used to sending all blacks through the service entrance.

The presence of DePriest was particularly moving for African-Americans on the White House staff who served the wives at the tea. According to information in Hoover's papers, the chief usher called DePriest the most "dignified woman in the room." Unfortunately, DePriest did not leave a record of her experience at the White House that day, but when her husband was asked about it not long after, he confirmed that his wife was treated respectfully and quipped, "All the negroes want is a square deal. And a tea isn't even a square meal."

Historically, wives of prominent black men have been highly educated, staunchly in the upper or middle class, and almost always light-skinned. Also, more often than not, they have been of a higher social and/or educational class than their husbands. Black leaders

A'Lelia Walker (1885–1931), daughter of Madam C.J. Walker and heiress to her fortune, at home in her 136th Street townhouse, also known as the Dark Tower, in the 1920s. Langston Hughes famously called her the "joy goddess" of Harlem thanks to the legendary parties she hosted there.

like Booker T. Washington, W.E.B. Du Bois, and early black politicians were all married to women who fit the bill. There were also black women married to prominent black men who were accomplished in their own right; in the case of women like Ida B. Wells-Barnett, Mary Church Terrell, Fannie Barrier Williams, and Victoria Earle Matthews, history would know their names better than their husbands. They were also interested in keeping up appearances—publicly and privately—especially considering the pressure of representing "Negro Womanhood" to America and the world at large. In Deborah Gray White's *Too Heavy A Load: Black Women in Defense of Themselves, 1894–1994*, the historian noted the scarcity of personal details in some of the subjects of her book, the early black club women who would lay the foundation for civil rights and women's rights in the late 19th and early 20th century. White wrote about the reticence that Mary Church Terrell (1863–1954) had in writing about her personal life in her memoir, *A Colored Woman in a White World* (1940), saying:

> Most of them were cautious about putting their private lives and histories in the hands of a media that had for centuries stereotyped and slandered black women. Rather than take such a risk, black women learned to practice what historian Darlene Clark Hine called the art of dissemblance. They let their public see only what they wanted them to see. As far as their audience was concerned, the public was the private.

As a result, most of these women would leave public rather than private memorabilia. This sense of responsibility would continue well into the 20th century for many, but not all, black women in the public eye.

"The colored Elsa Maxwell"

At the peak of the Harlem Renaissance, Geraldyn Dismond (1894-1984), later much better known as Gerri Major, was the managing editor of the first "gossipy black weekly," the *Inter-State Tatler*. And she had a lot to report on: from some of the first recorded black drag balls to the latest party at Madam C.J. Walker heiress A'Lelia Walker's townhouse on 136th Street, nicknamed "the Dark Tower." ("Bacchus himself passed out before midnight…" she raved about one bash in 1929.) A University of Chicago graduate born in Chicago in 1894, Major was also a reporter for other African American newspapers like *The New York Amsterdam News* and was married to Dr. Henry Binga Dismond (the first of three husbands), a track-and-field star at the University of Chicago who was also a pioneer in x-ray technology and physical therapy. The Dismonds lived on Harlem's storied "Striver's Row," a block of townhouses on West 139th Street known for its affluent residents. Known for her grand style and joie de vivre, Major was sometimes called "Harlem's Hostess," because she hosted so many glamorous parties in her home.

The *Tatler* included columns like "About People You Know," "Club Scribblings," "The World, the Flesh, and the Devil," and "Between Puffs," a column she wrote under the byline "Lady Nicotine." Her detailed reporting on the Harlem scene "made it difficult for anyone to party anonymously." After leaving the *Tatler*, she became a publicity agent and opened the Geraldyn Dismond Bureau of Specialized Publicity, on 135th Street in Harlem. Decades later, she would become known as the globe-trotting society editor of *Jet* magazine, a position she held for more than 30 years. She was also the author, with Doris E. Saunders, of *Black Society*, an expansive history of black society from the 18th century to the book's publication in 1977.

Hollywood wives

Wives of any color in Hollywood have always been in a delicate position, at the side of highly visible husbands who were rich or handsome—or both. Some knew how to navigate a sometimes complicated set of people and circumstances that could affect their husbands' careers and their own standing in the small, tight-knit community of the motion picture capitol of the world. As Donald Bogle chronicled in his book, *Bright Boulevards, Bold Dreams: The Story of Black Hollywood* (2005), Geri Branton and her best friend, Dorothy Dandridge, really loved hosting parties when they were married to the Nicholas brothers, Fayard and Harold, respectively. This was about a decade before Dorothy would reach true stardom and, according to Branton, Dorothy and Harold's huge backyard was the place where they would host barbecues and parties for stars like Billie Holiday, Cab Calloway, and Count Basie and his entire band when they came to town. Branton also knew that every guest was not an actual friend. "They knew I knew other stars. And they used that. This is a *using* town. You have no worth if you can't produce." Some wives were higher up the totem pole than others. Hyacinth Curtis, an original Cotton Club dancer and wife of Clarence Robinson, choreographer of the classic film *Stormy Weather*, told dance historian Brenda Dixon-Gottschild, "He was never given a contract for anything else... If he had been white, I wouldn't be sitting here today, I'd be rich. Because any time you do a musical like that you don't look back anymore... you go on." Many were in and out of the headlines with every up and down of their marriages—and subsequent divorces—like June Eckstine, the first wife of singer Billy Eckstine, and Marva Louis, the much photographed first wife of boxing legend Joe Louis. Born Marva Trotter in Boley, Oklahoma in 1915 (d. 2000), and raised in Chicago, she was a stenographer when she met Louis. Hours after their wedding on September 24, 1935, she was in the audience cheering him on at his boxing match. Always glamorous, Marva was a popular subject in black newspapers and magazines of the day and was an early champion of the iconic photographer Gordon Parks. She was popular enough to remain in the headlines of the black press even after she married and divorced Louis twice. She was also very creative, designing and making her own clothes and trying her hand as a singer for a few years in the mid-1940s, appearing with the likes of Duke Ellington and Count Basie.

Maria Cole (1922–2012), born Maria Hawkins, was raised by her aunt, the venerable educator Charlotte Hawkins Brown (1883–1961), and grew up on the campus of Palmer Memorial Institute, the school Dr. Brown founded in 1911. They lived in a two-story house called "Canary Cottage" because of its bright yellow color. Growing up in Dr. Brown's household allowed Maria to meet luminaries such as W.E.B. Du Bois, Mary McLeod Bethune, and Eleanor Roosevelt when they came to visit the school. Although Dr. Brown allowed Hawkins to take piano and voice lessons, she was not happy with her niece's interest in the entertainment business. To say that women raised under the watchful eyes of the old black middle class had a lot of pressure placed on them would be an understatement. Every dress, every hairstyle, every achievement was a political statement, a stake through the heart of injustice. Actress and writer Ellen Holly noted in her memoir how she and other unmarried women of her set were "as closely guarded as the daughters of Spanish aristocrats watched over by duennas."

While attending Boston Clerical College, Hawkins moved to New York for a month one summer when Blanche Calloway hired her as a replacement singer in her band. She wanted to stay in New York and nearly got permission to do so from her father when her aunt called in a favor to Mordecai Johnson, president of Howard University. Still displeased with Hawkins' pursuit of a career in entertainment, Brown secured a clerical job for her niece at the school. Hawkins didn't last long in Washington, D.C., though, and was soon back in New York singing with jazz icon Benny Carter (using the stage name Marie Winter so word would not get back to her aunt). In 1943, she married a Tuskegee Airman named Spurgeon Ellington, who was killed during a routine training flight shortly after World War II ended in December 1945. She sang briefly under her married name Ellington with the most famous Ellington of all, joining Joya Sherrill and Kay Davis to form a singing trio with Duke Ellington. By 1946, she was dismissed by Ellington when he learned that she planned a solo career, and she started singing in nightclubs. She met Nat "King" Cole in one of those nightclubs soon after and they were married on Easter Sunday 1948 at the famous Abyssinian Baptist Church in Harlem by Adam Clayton Powell, Jr. Their daughter Carole "Cookie" Cole would later say that her mother "radically altered" the famous crooner's style. She replaced his zoot suits with the classic, bespoke pieces that were to be his trademark. After Nat "King" Cole died in 1965, Maria Cole founded the Cole Cancer Foundation and produced the Broadway production of James Baldwin's *The Amen Corner*.

Born in Miami and raised on the campus of Bethune-Cookman College in Daytona Beach, Florida, Edna Mae Robinson (1916–2002), who would be married for 19 years to boxing legend Sugar Ray Robinson, graduated from high school when she was only 14. After moving to New York, she danced at the Cotton Club and toured with Duke Ellington and Cab Calloway in Europe. She gave up her career after marrying Robinson in 1943 and, according to their son, Ray Robinson, Jr., she helped him fine-tune his image for the public. "Dad was put together by my mother and her stepmother. They taught him how to speak, how to walk, how to dress, what to wear, they even laid out his clothing for him. They took a rough stone and polished it into a jewel." She also opened businesses with him in Harlem, including Golden Gloves Barber Shop, Sugar Ray's Quality Cleaners, and a boutique called Edna Mae's Lingerie. Edna Robinson also had the distinction of being on the cover of the very first issue of *Jet* magazine. The Robinsons divorced in 1962 and in later years Edna Robinson would serve as a technical consultant on Francis Ford Coppola's 1983 film, *The Cotton Club*, as well as teach dance and aerobics to seniors.

Camille Cosby (b. 1945) had an epiphany in her thirties that led her to return to school almost 20 years after she'd dropped out of the University of Maryland as a sophomore to marry Bill Cosby. "Looking back on those years, I don't think that I thought I was smart," she said in a 2000 interview for the inaugural issue of *O, The Oprah Magazine*. "I knew I was a good mother, but I didn't think that I was smart in terms of having something to say if Bill and I were seated with a group of people who were busy doing their different things. I always said, 'My husband is the public person. He is the one who has something to say.' I never felt I had anything to contribute, something that people would want to hear." She would later say that going back to school and earning a master's and then a doctoral degree helped her self-esteem grow. Dr. Cosby would go on to produce hit television and Broadway versions of the book, *Having Our Say*, about the lives of centenarian sisters Dr. Annie (Bessie) Delany and teacher Sarah Delany. "Education helped me to come out of myself, to come out of the home, because I had been raising my children. Not that that is a bad thing; it is the most difficult job I have ever had. But that was just one part of my womanness. I had to fulfill myself in other ways, to pursue my interests, to know that I could do many things."

III/1

MARVA LOUIS

Strolling with her new husband, Joe Louis, in Harlem in 1935.

III/2

MARVA LOUIS

Stenographer turned model and singer (1915–2000), the first wife of boxing legend Joe Louis, seen stepping into a Duesenberg Roadster in Harlem's Sugar Hill on June 18, 1936. Hours later, her husband would lose to Max Schmeling at Yankee Stadium in one of the most famous bouts in boxing history. Louis would go on to defeat Schmeling in a rematch on June 22, 1938.

III/3

EDNA ROBINSON

The former entertainer (1916–2002), with husband, boxing legend Sugar Ray Robinson, at the movie premiere of *The Prince and the Showgirl* at Radio City Music Hall in New York City on June 14, 1957.

III/4

EDNA ROBINSON

Cheering on her husband as he fought
Jake LaMotta on February 14, 1951.

III/5

MARIA COLE

The former singer (1922–2012) trying on one of her gifts at a party in Harlem celebrating her marriage to Nat "King" Cole in March 1948.

III/6

MARIA COLE

With husband, Nat, arriving at the Academy Awards in Los Angeles in 1963.

III/7

JUNE ECKSTINE

June Eckstine applies lipstick as her husband, popular jazz singer Billy Eckstine, adjusts his tie at a dressing table in their Manhattan apartment on April 11, 1950. The Eckstines, who divorced two years later, were photographed for *Life* magazine by Martha Holmes.

III/8

CAMILLE COSBY

Arriving at the Emmy Awards in Los Angeles in September 1965, Camille (b. 1945) and her husband, Bill. The Cosbys would go on to earn doctorates in education from the University of Massachusetts at Amherst.

BEAUTY & FASHION ENTREPRENEURS

THE INSPIRATION FOR DUKE ELLINGTON'S ONLY OPERA, *Queenie Pie*, Madam C.J. Walker was born Sarah Breedlove in Delta, Louisiana in 1867. As a widow with a young child, she moved to be closer to her brothers, who worked as barbers, and took work as a laundress. It was during this time that she started having problems with her hair and scalp, problems that were directly attributable to a lack of indoor plumbing and electricity, which was common in the United States at the time. Since most Americans went without indoor plumbing, bathing was rare and shampooing hair even more so, which meant that people often went bald or were vulnerable to environmental hazards such as pollution, bacteria, and lice. After some experimentation, she discovered an ointment and developed a cleansing regimen that healed her scalp. Her hair began to grow again and the idea for her business was born. After marrying a newspaper salesman named Charles Joseph Walker, she adopted the name "Madam" C.J. Walker. The moniker was inspired by the women who had created the French cosmetics and fashion industries. It was also a handy tool to command respect in an era when black adults were called by their first names, even by children. (Many blacks would give their children names like General, Major, Sergeant, and Mister to address this issue.) Walker would go on to build a factory to make her products, along with a salon and a beauty school where her proud sales force of former sharecroppers, maids, and teachers were trained. She also expanded her brand to places like Jamaica, Costa Rica, Haiti, and Panama. She enjoyed the fruits of her success by buying a beautiful Victorian mansion in Irvington-on-Hudson, New York and having it designed by Vertner Woodson Tandy, the first African-American registered architect in the State of New York. Walker was also very sensitive to charges that she was encouraging black women to look white in any way and, while she was alive, the Walker Company never sold skin bleach and the words "hair straightener" never appeared in any of the company's advertisements. She told one newspaper in 1918, "Right here, let me correct the erroneous impression held by some that I claim to straighten hair. I deplore such an impression because I have always held myself out as a hair culturist. I grow hair."

Rose Morgan (1912–2008) styling her friend and client Margaret Tynes in the mid-1950s.

In the tradition of Madam Walker, black hairstylists have always been some of the earliest successful black entrepreneurs. Madam Walker may still be the best known to later generations, but there have been many examples over the years of successful black women across the United States in the hair business. One example is Louise Scott (1905–1983) of New Jersey. Born in South Carolina, she arrived in Newark, New Jersey in 1940 to work as a domestic during the day while studying at night to become a beautician. After graduation, she opened her first beauty salon and, soon after, had four more salons, a guesthouse, and a hotel. In 1959, she purchased the Krueger Mansion, a Victorian-era, 26-room mansion built between 1887 and 1889 by Gottfried Krueger, the German-born mogul behind Krueger Breweries, the first major brewery to sell beer in a can. Scott maintained the mansion, which was later renamed the Krueger-Scott Mansion, as both her private home and the headquarters of her Scott College of Beauty Culture. Another Newark beauty and style pioneer was Emily Miles (1909–1998), the founder of the Belle Meade Models. Well known and revered throughout her long life for her unrelenting sense of style and taste, she ran Belle Meade for more than five decades, not only training models and producing extravagant shows but also coaching beauty contestants, debutantes, and men and women of all ages for various social occasions.

The most high-profile beauty entrepreneur of this era was Rose Morgan (1912–2008), owner of the Rose-Meta House of Beauty in Harlem. A former wife of boxing legend

Joe Louis, her celebrity clientele (long before her marriage) included Lena Horne, Ethel Waters, and my aunt, Margaret Tynes. Enamored of New York City, Morgan moved there permanently after a stay in town to do Ethel Water's hair. Within a year, she hired half a dozen stylists and opened a salon at 401 West 148th Street in Harlem with her business partner, Olivia Clarke Stanford. The salon eventually expanded to include a dressmaking department, a charm school, and a wig salon. In 1965, Morgan was a co-founder of the black-owned Freedom National Bank in New York. During fashion shows at the Rose-Meta House of Beauty, which usually featured employees and clients as models, rose-scented cologne wafted through the air. The fashion shows were also designed to promote African-American milliners like Willard Winter and Mildred Blount (1907–1974), who designed most of the hats for the classic film *Gone with the Wind* among several others. Blount also boasted a private clientele that included film legends like Mary Pickford, Rosalind Russell, Joan Crawford, and Marlene Dietrich as well as Katherine Dunham. She also gained notice for designing the wedding veil for an heiress known to my generation for her designer jeans: Gloria Vanderbilt.

Ophelia DeVore (1922–2014) did not plan on becoming a modeling pioneer, especially when the modeling business itself was so new and uncertain. The South Carolina-born beauty arrived in New York to further her education and began modeling after being encouraged by friends who were impressed with her photographs. As she told *Ebony*, "I had a background in dancing, piano, and all the other things in the arts that parents gave you to make you a lady." She enrolled in the Vogue School of Modeling (not affiliated with the magazine) and took classes on modeling and charm, unaware that the school did not know that she was black. It was only when she witnessed the bewilderment of school officials at the arrival of another black model with café-au-lait skin that she realized the school didn't know that they already had a black model. "I didn't know that they didn't know. I thought they knew what I was." According to DeVore, her own brief modeling career mainly consisted of working with *Ebony* magazine. "I didn't go for modeling jobs, I just happened to be recommended by people at *Ebony* magazine, some of the salespeople who were my friends." Her friends also saw something else in DeVore—the potential to use modeling as a way of showing a positive image of black people in a media landscape that insisted upon dealing in garish stereotypes. This appealed to DeVore, who always had an eye on improving the image of black people in the media and, in 1946, she and four friends began the Grace Del Marco Modeling Agency. "Grace" signaled elegance and style, and "Marco" was an acronym formed by the names of its founders: "M" from Marie Mayo; "A" from Albert Murphy; "R" from Rupert Callendar; "C" from Charles Mayo; and "O" from Ophelia DeVore (and "Del" from the Spanish for "by"). Many of DeVore's models had great success, but the most successful was Helen Williams, who was easily one of the most photographed black models of the 1950s and 1960s. Williams appeared in advertisements for brands like Kodak and Bulova. At the height of her career, she made $35 an hour, unprecedented for a black model in those days. The charm school component of Grace Del Marco began in 1948 with lessons in etiquette, speech, drama, ballet, modeling, and "Positive Mental Attitude." A teenaged Carol Diane Johnson, who would later become Diahann Carroll, passed through the school as she was modeling for *Ebony* and competed in beauty contests. Cicely Tyson, while doing a bit of modeling herself, trained models and actors at the school.

DeVore was fearless in her advocacy for fair treatment for black models and she was never hesitant to speak out if she felt her models—or her business—were being unfairly treated or paid. She once sued *LIFE* magazine for "rewriting" the history of blacks in the modeling

Charlotte Hawkins Brown (1883–1961) on her wedding day in 1911. In her 1941-published book of etiquette written expressly for African-Americans, *The Correct Thing: To Do, To Say, To Wear*, she dispensed essential advice on the appropriate fashion to be worn at any social occasion, as well as how to properly behave. Some of it remains suprprisingly relevant. A pioneering educator, aged just 19 she converted a blacksmith's shop into Palmer Memorial Institute, a day and boarding school for African-Americans. She went on to lecture at top colleges including Smith, Radcliffe, Howard, Hampton and the Tuskegee Institute.

business after a 1971 article on the boom of black models in the industry only cited white-owned agencies, many of whom lured their black models from Grace Del Marco and other black agencies. Ms. DeVore told *Jet* in 1971 that *LIFE* intentionally highlighted the white agencies "who have not devoted the years of struggle and sacrifice to train, develop, guide and direct Black models for business contacts like I have been doing for twenty-five years." Those 25 years turned to over 50 years in business, during which DeVore expanded into a cosmetics line and also owned a newspaper for several decades. "I didn't model a long time because that wasn't my mission to be a model. My mission was to have us presented in a way that was not stereotyped."

Fashion

A decade after Ann Lowe (1898–1981) created her most famous dress, the wedding gown Jacqueline Bouvier wore when she married Senator John F. Kennedy in 1953, Lowe described herself to *Ebony*'s society editor, Gerri Major, as "an awful snob… I love my clothes and I'm particular about who wears them. I do not cater to Mary and Sue." Lowe was from Alabama and famous for designing gowns and cocktail dresses for several prominent New York society families with legendary names like Rockefeller, Post, and du Pont. Her career began under sad circumstances when she was just 16. Her mother, Jane Lowe, left four unfinished gowns for Emmett O'Neal, the first lady of Alabama, when she died in 1914. Ann finished the gowns for Mrs. O'Neal and embarked on what would be a five-decade career designing and sewing exclusively for wealthy clients. In 1916, she moved to New York for a year to attend the S.L. Taylor School of Design. She lamented to her family that she had a hard time in New York, and as the only black person there, she was forced by school officials to sit in a room away from her classmates. In 1919, after her second marriage, she opened Annie Cohen Designs. Her shop was a success but her marriage faltered. She joked to friends that her husband wanted a "real wife, not someone who was forever jumping out of bed to sketch." By 1928 she was calling herself Ann Lowe again and had saved $19,000, which she used to open a third-floor loft on Lexington Avenue in Manhattan. By 1965, she was in her own atelier at 540 Madison Avenue. Her designs were also sold at Henri Bendel in New York City and at Neiman Marcus in Dallas, Texas. Lowe's creations were truly custom-made and, to be certain that her dresses did not look too much alike, she cut a swatch of material with and filed it with the sketch so it would not be repeated. She was at the height of her career when she designed the silk chiffon bridal gown for Jacqueline Bouvier Kennedy. She specialized in working with the finest fabrics, and handmade flowers and beadwork were her trademarks. The Kennedy gown required 50 yards of ivory silk taffeta and took more than two months to make. She also designed the pink silk gowns and matching Tudor caps worn by the bridesmaids. The wedding was covered extensively in the press, of course, but Ann Lowe did not get instant mainstream fame because most papers, including the *New York Times* in their expansive coverage of the wedding, gave extensive details of every inch of Kennedy's gown—without mentioning the designer by name. But that didn't really matter too much to Mrs. Lowe since she preferred her clientele to stay exactly as it was—*exclusive*. Incidentally, the late John F. Kennedy, Jr. commissioned a black designer named Gordon Henderson to make the suit for his wedding, and his sister Caroline Kennedy's groom, Edward Schlossberg, would wear a navy suit made by black designer Willi Smith.

Zelda Wynn Valdes' unapologetically sexy, hip-hugging gowns were worn by celebrities and celebrity wives like Dorothy Dandridge, Josephine Baker, Ella Fitzgerald, Joyce Bryant,

Maria Cole, and Edna Robinson, and later superstars like Gladys Knight and opera diva Jessye Norman. She also designed dresses for legendary figures like Marlene Dietrich and Mae West. In 1948, Valdes (1905–2001) opened her own boutique in Manhattan in what is now Washington Heights, on Broadway and West 158th Street. She later moved "Chez Zelda" midtown to 57th Street, where her sister, Mary Barbour, assisted her and supervised the staff of the store that attracted celebrities and stylish women from all walks of life. In 1949, she was president of the New York chapter of NAFAD, the National Association of Fashion and Accessory Designers, an organization of black designers that was founded by the iconic educator Mary McLeod Bethune.

One of the black stars dressed by Valdes was Joyce Bryant (see Chapter VI). She was dubbed "the Black Marilyn Monroe" and was best known for her sexy image, which was jumpstarted by Valdes. In 1953, *Our World*, a popular magazine for African-Americans, noted that, "Zelda's gowns changed torch singer Joyce Bryant's career." When Valdes met Bryant, the performer was wearing bouffant, "sweet" dresses and was singing "sweet" songs, which, as the designer noted, she preferred because she was religious. However, Valdes convinced the singer that hiding her curves wasn't doing her any favors. Once Bryant adopted the skintight, low-cut gowns of Zelda Wynn Valdes, her career took off.

In 1960 Valdes designed the first and original costume for Playboy club hostesses (the "bunny" outfit). In 1970, Arthur Mitchell asked Valdes to design costumes for his year-old dance company, the Dance Theater of Harlem, and she stayed for 30 years and became the company's matriarch until her death in 2001 at the age of 96. "I just had a God-given talent for making people beautiful," she said in a 1994 interview—and she was being modest. Consider the story that she always told about Ella Fitzgerald: "Edna Robinson (Sugar Ray Robinson's wife) recommended me to Ms. Fitzgerald when she was going to sing at the Apollo Theater in New York. I was able to measure her once, but thereafter she was so busy that she didn't have the time. She would order—always in a rush—and I would study photos of her and guess her increasing size. She always said they fit and she'd order more, always three at a time. I never had more than three to four days to finish the gowns. I am pleased to say that I never missed a delivery."

IV/1

OPHELIA DEVORE

Businesswoman, publisher and model (1922–2014), photogaphed in the 1940s.

IV/2

OPHELIA DEVORE

Seen at the 1954 Miss Rheingold beauty contest (seated) talking with potential contestants. One of her models, Helen Williams, would later recall how DeVore pushed her models to enter the popular pageant despite perceived racial bias.

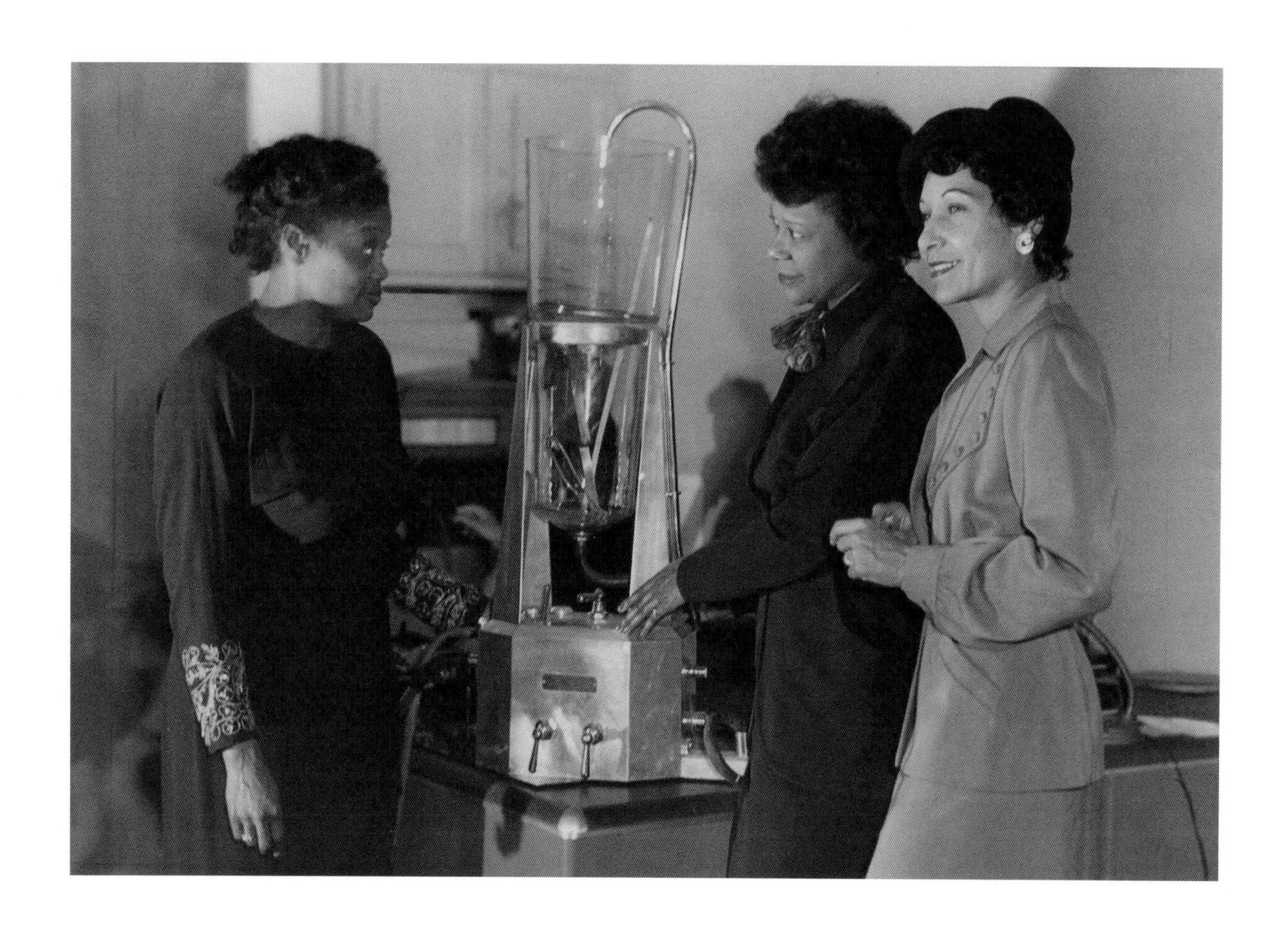

IV/3

ROSE MORGAN

Rose Morgan (1912–2008) and her business partner, Olivia Clarke Stanford (far right), presenting a gift to Robin Bennett (left) for Mt. Morris Park Hospital in Harlem.

IV/4

ROSE MORGAN

Margaret Tynes (left, in fur) and Rose Morgan (right) at a 1957 NAACP Freedom Fund dinner in honor of Duke Ellington and Branch Rickey, the baseball executive who brought Jackie Robinson to Major League Baseball. They are joined by (from left) New York governor W. Averell Harriman, entertainer Steve Allen, Robinson and Cab Calloway.

PRIMA DONNAS ASSOLUTAS

OPERA AND DANCE

LURANAH ALDRIDGE (1860–1932), a "strong-willed, dominating, and pleasure-loving woman," (as the *New Yorker* descrivbed her in 2013) was possibly on the verge of a remarkable career that may have mirrored that of her father, Ira Aldridge, the pioneering Shakespearean actor who astounded European audiences in the mid-19th century. At the age of 36, she was set to appear at the Bayreuth Festival in Germany to perform *Ring of the Nibelung* by Richard Wagner before she became sick during rehearsals and could not go on. Even with the support of Wagner's widow, Cosima, a powerful figure in the music scene at the time, Aldridge never appeared onstage. Her sister Amanda, a friend of W.E.B. Du Bois, was a singer, composer, and a voice teacher whose students included three future icons: Roland Hayes, Paul Robeson, and Marian Anderson. Had Aldridge been better known, she might have served as an inspiration for generations of opera singers to come.

Lillian Evanti (1890–1967) emerged in the early 20th century and was a darling of the black elite, the educated, powerful blacks who preferred more high-end types of entertainment like classical music and opera over what they saw as the rough-hewn vaudeville and, later, ragtime and jazz music. Born Annie Lillian Evans in Washington, D.C. to a teacher and a doctor, she graduated from Howard University in 1917. She spoke and sang in five languages. She changed her last name to Evanti, which blended her last name with that of her husband, Howard University professor Roy Tibbs, at the suggestion of her friend, the Harlem Renaissance poet and novelist Jessie Fauset. Evanti would later gain prominence in Europe before returning to the United States after the start of World War II to found the National Negro Opera Company.

In subsequent generations, marquee names like Marian Anderson and Leontyne Price would have a prominent place in U.S. operatic history and the history of black entertainment, but there were also many singers who would gain more prominence overseas. They weren't superstars, but their successes contributed to the chipping away of barriers that would hold black artists back for decades. Mattiwilda Dobbs, Gloria Davy, Reri Grist, Muriel Rahn, Felicia Weathers, Anne Brown, and Margaret Tynes were among them.

The elegant contralto Marian Anderson (1897–1993) photographed in the early 1940s by Morgan and Marvin Smith. The Philadelphia-born Anderson was the first African-American to sing at the Metropolitan Opera, although she is probably best known to many for singing before a crowd of 75,000 at the Lincoln Memorial in Washington, D.C. in 1939. After the Daughters of the American Revolution refused to permit her to sing at Constitution Hall, DAR made the effort to make up for the slight, inviting Anderson to sing at the hall on many occasions after the infamous incident.

Dance

Katherine Dunham (1909–2006) laid it on the line in plain terms: "I admit that a strong sociological purpose motivates my work and that there is a real drive in my purpose to present good-looking, talented, clean, healthy-minded, and healthy-bodied young American Negroes in a repertoire of dance mimes and sketches. How well I am succeeding is well illustrated by incidents both in this country and Mexico, where, during our last tour, I was invited with the members of my company to call on President Miguel Aleman, who was most gracious in praise of our performance. He was particularly pleased that we spoke to him in Spanish, such as it was, an effrontery in view of his good English, but one that broke the contretemps and established a friendly feeling at once. Our appearance in Mexico, for example, did much to counteract Holly's cliché's for the Negro. They discovered that the Negro can also be an artist and not always a shiftless, ignorant person. Miguel Covarrubias brought his students to the theater where we were performing to sketch Dunham dancers. They expressed surprise at the intelligence and the artistry of my dancers."

Dunham formed Ballet Nègre, one of the first black ballet companies in the United States, in 1930, and studied the dances of Jamaica, Trinidad, and Haiti as a part of her anthropological fieldwork. In 1938, Dunham choreographed and produced her first

full-length ballet, L'Ag'Ya, based on a fable of love, jealousy, and revenge culminating in a staged version of the ag'ya, the fighting dance of Martinique. Using a pseudonym, Kaye Dunn, Dunham wrote two articles for *Esquire* magazine in 1939, "La Boule Blanche" and "L'Ag'ya of Martinique." The illustrations for the articles were by E. Simms Campbell.

Katherine Dunham (1909–2006) photographed in 1946.

Janet Collins was born in New Orleans in 1917 and raised in Los Angeles in a family that was supportive of her creative endeavors. "Mama didn't interfere," she told biographer Yael Tamar Lewin in 2003, a few months before her death at the age of 86. "Because she always arranged the activity of the home around the fact I had to practice, and I had to paint." The woman who would become the first black prima ballerina at The Metropolitan Opera in New York in 1951 was nearly the first black ballerina with the prestigious Ballet Russe de Monte Carlo, when she was only 15. But she turned the job down when she was told that she would have to paint herself white. She studied dance with Lester Horton and Katherine Dunham, appearing in the 1943 film *Stormy Weather* with the Dunham troupe.

Collins also appeared in the 1946 film *The Thrill of Brazil*, which featured her in the "Rendezvous in Rio" macumba. "The reason I became ballerina of the Metropolitan Opera was because I couldn't be topped. You don't get there because, you get there in spite of." Collins always had an air of mystery about her, even to her own family. Her cousin Carmen de Lavallade said, "Janet was rather like Auntie Mame… she'd just breeze into town because she danced with Katherine Dunham's company. And when she came into town, it was really something—and then she'd breeze out again. She was a fascinating woman."

Carmen de Lavallade's own career would take on a higher profile than her cousin's, due in no small part to growing opportunities for theater performers to appear on television. Born in 1931 in Los Angeles, she was raised by an aunt who owned and operated an African-American bookstore. Her dance career began with the Lester Horton Dance Group. It was in Los Angeles in 1950 that Lena Horne saw her perform with the Lester Horton dance troupe and was impressed by the *soignée* de Lavallade. The dancer quickly agreed to Horton's request to sponsor her. Sponsorship entailed small things that would amount to big returns, such as strategic photo ops and press releases to the media—and Horne also introduced the 19-year-old beauty to executives at 20th Century Fox.

By 1955, de Lavallade had appeared in four movies, including in the fast-paced nightclub dance sequence in *Carmen Jones*. That sequence also featured her fellow Horton dancer and lifelong friend Alvin Ailey, as well as the drummer Max Roach. She met her future husband, Geoffrey Holder, when they both appeared as dancers in Truman Capote's Broadway musical *House of Flowers* in 1954. Their wedding in June 1955 was held on the estate of theater maven Lucille Lortel in Westport, Connecticut and attended by a host of luminaries from the worlds of theater, dance, art, and literature.

The following year, de Lavallade succeeded Collins as prima ballerina of the Metropolitan Opera and then made the first of many television appearances with John Butler's ballet, *Flight*, in 1956, followed by Duke Ellington's *A Drum Is a Woman* in 1957. In later years she reemerged on Broadway and become a full professor at Yale and a member of the Yale Repertory Theater. One of the classes she taught at Yale was called "Movement to Actors" and she counted Meryl Streep among her students. In 2014, she began rehearsals for "As I Remember It," a show that she co-created about her life told through dance, film, and her personal writing.

V/1

LEONTYNE PRICE

A legendary lirico-spinto soprano, Price (b. 1927) was photographed here by Carl Van Vechten in 1953. Born Mary Violet Price in Laurel, Mississippi to a mother who was a midwife and a carpenter father, she was given a piano at the age of 3 after showing remarkable musical talent. A graduate of Central State University, Ohio, she earned the support of Paul Robeson, who sang for the scholarship fund that enabled her to attended Julliard. Her professional debut was in 1952, and later that year she toured the U.S. and Europe in a revival of *Porgy And Bess*. After rejecting the role of *Aida* at the Met in 1958, she debuted there in 1960 as the lead in *Il Trovatore*, earning the longest ovation in the history of the Opera House. She has won 13 Grammy Awards and countless other honors throughout her career.

V/2

LEONTYNE PRICE & HILDA SIMMS

Actor Hilda Simms (1918–1994, right) meeting Leontyne Price (b. 1927), possibly at the time of Price's appearance as Bess in *Porgy and Bess* (1952).

V/3

ELISABETH WELCH

An American singer (1904–2003) photographed in 1935, she introduced the Charleston on Broadway before becoming a superstar in the U.K. Born in Manhattan to a Scottish-Irish mother and African-American father, Welch was a favorite of iconic composers Noël Coward and Cole Porter. She was the first singer to popularize the classic Porter tune "Love for Sale," and it became a signature song for her. She also introduced "Stormy Weather" to British audiences and became so beloved in the U.K. that she remained there for the rest of her life. Among other highlights in her 70-year career, Ms. Welch was nominated for a Tony Award for Best Featured Actress in a Musical in 1986 at age 82, for her role in *Jerome Kern Goes to Hollywood*. Welch also starred in two films with Paul Robeson, *Song of Freedom* in 1936 and *Big Fella* in 1937.

V/4

SHIRLEY VERRETT

New Orleans–born and Los Angeles–raised mezzo-soprano, photographed in 1961 by Carl Van Vechten. Verrett (1931–2010) appeared at major opera houses around the world between 1958 and 1994.

V/5

GLORIA DAVY

A Brooklyn-born lirico-spinto soprano, Davy (1931–2012) was the first black performer to sing the lead in *Aida* at the New York Met, in 1958. This photograph was taken that year by Carl Van Vechten.

v/6

RERI GRIST

A New York born and bred coloratura soprano (b. 1932), Grist was photographed by Carl Van Vechten in 1959. That year she made her first professional appearance in Santa Fe as Adele in *Die Fledermaus*. She spent much of the following decade singing in Europe, although she made her first New York Met appearance in 1966. That was nine years after debuting the song "Somewhere" in the original Broadway production of Sondheim and Bernstein's *West Side Story*.

V/7

MURIEL SMITH

Born in New York, Smith (1923–1985) was the first black singer to study at the Curtis Institute of Music in Philadelphia—on a scholarship arranged after she won an amateur radio talent show in 1937. In 1943 she was the lead in *Carmen Jones* when it debuted on Broadway. She remained with the show for three years and moved to the U.K. in 1949, making her operatic debut as the lead in *Carmen* in 1955 at London's Royal Opera House, Covent Garden. She rejected a part in the movie version of *Porgy And Bess* in 1959 because, she said, "It doesn't do the right thing for my people." Photographed here in 1944 by Carl Van Vechten.

v/8

MURIEL RAHN

A Boston-born singer, Rahn (1911–1961) alternated the role of *Carmen Jones* with Muriel Smith in 1949. Ten years later she became the first black musical director of a theatre in Frankfurt, Germany. Photographed in 1944, by Carl Van Vechten.

V/9

KATHERINE DUNHAM

The legendary choreographer and dancer with two of her troupe and the actor and singer Tony Martin, in the 1948 film *Casbah*.

V/10

PEARL PRIMUS

"Dance has been my freedom and my world." Trinidadian Primus (1919–1994) is best known for creating dances like "Strange Fruit" and "The Negro Speaks of Rivers," which were inspired by poetry and social issues. After earning a biology degree from Hunter College, she won a prestigious Julius Rosenwald grant and used it to study African dance throughout the continent of Africa, especially in Nigeria, Zaire, Rwanda, and Ghana. In 1978, she earned a Ph.D. in anthropology from New York University and taught dance for the rest of her life. Photographed here in 1943 by Carl Van Vechten.

V/11

JANET COLLINS

Dancer Janet Collins (1917–2003) photographed by Carl Van Vechten in 1949. Two years later, she would become the first Black prima ballerina at the Metropolitan Opera.

CARMEN DE LAVALLADE

Los Angeles–born de Lavallade (b. 1931) was raised by an aunt who owned an African-American bookstore and was mentored early in her career by Lena Horne. She made her Broadway debut alongside her friend, the great choreographer Alvin Ailey, in *House of Flowers* in 1954, and became prima ballerina at the Metropolitan Opera in 1955.

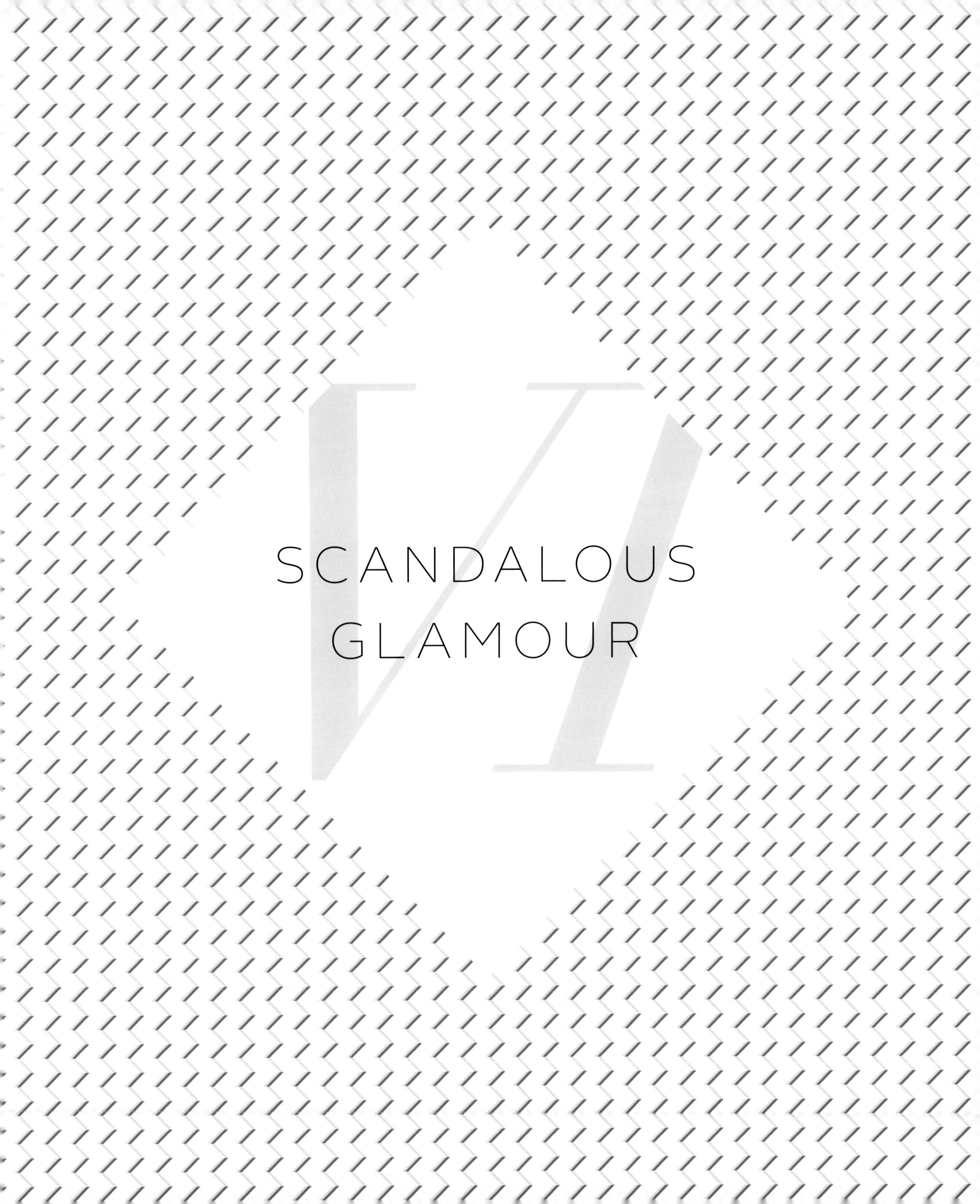

VI
SCANDALOUS GLAMOUR

NOT ALL OF THE EARLY GLAMOROUS black female pioneers felt pressured to conform to ideas of respectability. With her signature platinum blond hair and high-profile glamorous life that filled the gossip pages of her day, Nora Holt journeyed a long way from the Kansas she was born into in 1885 (d. 1974). She was born as Lena Douglas to Gracie Douglas, an educator, and Calvin Douglas, a prominent minister in the African Methodist Episcopal church. Reverend and Mrs. Douglas worked closely with Western University of Quindaro, the first all–African-American school west of the Mississippi River. Young Lena grew up on the school's campus, and in 1907, her father wrote the words to the school's official song and she composed the score. She would go on to become the first black person to receive a master's degree in music from Chicago Music College in 1918. However, it was rarely her impressive background that put her in gossip columns in the early 1920s. Holt may have seemed to be just another spoiled socialite, but it didn't particularly bother her, as she once wrote to her friend Carl Van Vechten during her nasty divorce in 1923, that the salacious headlines about her short-lived fourth marriage "should be of value" in generating publicity. "Nora, my dear, was something," my aunt Margaret Tynes recalled in a 2003 interview. "She was always doing something. Always!" Declared one of the "Most Married Negroes" by *Ebony* magazine in 1949, Holt had gained notoriety not only for her five tumultuous marriages but also for her radio show, *Nora Holt's Concert Showcase*, and her pivotal role as a music critic for the *New York Amsterdam News* in Harlem. She was also the inspiration for the "Lasca Sartoris" character in Van Vechten's infamous, controversial novel, *Nigger Heaven*.

But the most scandalous thing regarding Holt has to be the loss of over 200 of her musical compositions, which were stolen from the storage facility she had placed them in while she was vacationing in Europe. Only *Negro Dance, Opus 25, No. 1, for piano*, infused with elements of the blues and ragtime music, survives.

Joyce Bryant (b. 1928) in a custom gown by Zelda Wynn Valdes in May 1953. Photographed by Carl Van Vechten.

"Notoriety Papa"

Holt's secure financial position served as a buffer for her, something that eluded Gladys Bentley (1907–1960). Ostracized at home in Philadelphia by family, friends, and even doctors who wanted to "cure" her of homosexuality, Bentley was a 16-year-old renegade when she arrived in Harlem, eager to be free enough to be every aspect of herself. She started out singing at rent parties and, buoyed by her increasing popularity and distinctive style, she began performing in some of the most popular clubs in Harlem. She was unapologetically masculine in a top hat and tails or a simple man's suit, and her gleefully obscene set drew large crowds to her shows at the famous gay club the Clam House and other popular Harlem venues. Her salary increased considerably when coveted white patrons, including Carl Van Vechten, started coming to her shows. Soon, she was playing more mainstream venues like the Cotton Club and various white clubs downtown. As her star rose, a newspaper columnist wrote that Bentley had married her white girlfriend in a public ceremony in New Jersey. She was also the model for a blues performer in one of Van Vechten's novels, *Parties*. When playing to straight audiences Bentley made no concessions, and she continued to sing obscene songs and created salacious versions of popular numbers—although these elements were not present when she recorded for Okeh records in the late 1920s. However, in the 1950s, Bentley would denounce everything about her notorious career and declare that she was no longer a lesbian, thanks to female hormone treatments. She penned an article for *Ebony* called "I Am a Woman Again," where she spoke of being gay as a "personal hell."

She continued to perform, but her career waned, and just before she was to be ordained as a minister, she died of influenza at the age of 52.

"She fooled Hollywood"

Although Mildred Davenport, known professionally as "Acquanetta," was promoted as the "Venezuelan Volcano" and claimed Arapaho heritage, the July 1950 edition of the *Los Angeles Sentinel* described her as a "beautiful Negro screen actress." Like many starlets of the day, Acquanetta told different versions of her life story to the media. To the white press, she was the girl born as Burnu Acquanetta near Ozone, Wyoming in 1921, a member of the Arapaho tribe. In the Negro press, including a February 14, 1952 *Jet* cover story, she was breathlessly covered as the beautiful Mildred Davenport from Norristown, Pennsylvania, who left West Virginia State College for Negroes to start a career as a Broadway dancer. For most of her career—through marriages, births, divorces, the marriage of her sister Katherine, and the sad death of her four-year-old son, Sergio, in 1950—she was regularly covered by the Negro press as a black woman. She and members of her family are prominently featured in the collection of black twin-brother photographers Morgan (1910–1993) and Marvin (1910–2003) Smith.

What stopped her from telling the Negro press who followed her every move that she was not actually a "Negro" but an Arapaho, if that was in fact the case? It would be remarkable for an actress who was not black in the 1940s and 1950s to allow any media to cover her as a "Negro" when blacks were routinely denied even the smallest roles in white productions. But as late as 1998, she told the *Phoenix News Times* that her mother named her "Burnu Acquanetta" and that it meant "Burning Fire/Deep Water." She told the reporter that she was born in Cheyenne, Wyoming and that she was of Arapaho descent.

The July 1950 *Los Angeles Sentinel* story "Acquanetta Drops Suit" was about the actress abandoning an action against "Mexican-Jewish millionaire" Luciano Bashuk. The suit alleged that Bashuk, described as a wealthy importer, had married her and fathered her son, Sergio. No records of their Mexican marriage were recovered and the matter was dropped. In the 1998 interview, she alluded to her mysterious time in Mexico, after she broke a seven-year contract with Universal and her film career faded: "I didn't do it as something naughty, I just fell in love with Mexico when I visited there, so I decided not to come back. Then I got married, and had a little boy, Sergio, and then he died. I didn't love Mexico anymore, so I had to come back to the States." According to the August 22, 2004 edition of *The Arizona Republic*, Acquanetta's brother, then 85-year-old retired judge Horace A. Davenport, was present at her funeral. Judge Davenport, according to the Pennsylvania Bar Association, was "the first African-American judge in Montgomery County." He told the newspaper that he'd never seen any of his sister's movies.

"I was just a pound of flesh"

By all accounts, Joyce Bryant had real talent, but the media focus was on her sexy image, despite her impressive four-octave soprano voice. Once dubbed the "the Bronze Bombshell," she had enough mainstream success to do a photo spread in *LIFE* magazine. Constant mentions in Walter Winchell's gossip column made her a star and she was widely known as the first dark-skinned black woman to be considered a sex symbol inside and outside of the black community. In fact, she told the *New York Times* that she was "proud" of the fact that she was the first "identifiably black" woman to play the Copacabana in New York. According to Dorothy Dandridge's biographer Donald Bogle, Dandridge pulled Bryant aside after a date in still-segregated Miami Beach and asked for advice on negotiating her nightclub fees ("What do you do?") She was also very impressed with Bryant's stage presence, asking, "How do you walk up on that stage and stay as calm as you are? It seems to be so easy for you." Bryant earned nearly $1 million at her peak, but her upbringing in a very strict Seventh-Day Adventist home left her feeling guilty about sex and her image. Guilt and paranoia about her safety and her treatment by her management team brought things to a head in 1955, with signed contracts on the table for engagements from Las Vegas to Miami Beach. After she lost her voice following the removal of her tonsils, Bryant's manager brought a doctor to the dressing room and asked him to spray her throat with cocaine so she could make her performance. The doctor said no, telling her manager that she could become addicted. "I heard my manager say: 'I don't give a damn what you do. Just make her sing!' The bottom of my world fell out. I realized that I was just a pound of flesh. I said to the doctor, 'Thank you but no thank you. I hope I never have to see you again except as a fan.' Then I went on stage and did a fashion show—I wore gowns and whispered to the audience. When I finished the week, I said to my manager, 'I quit!' "

Bryant left show business at the top of her career and returned home and to the church, where she worked for 20 years, singing, ministering to the poor, and enduring sexism and lies from people who were less than forgiving about her past. Finally, disappointed with the people in her church, she left and eventually made her way back to the stage. After undertaking classical voice training she sang opera in Europe, South America, and with the New York Opera Company. She had a successful cabaret run in the late 1970s and 1980s in New York and worked as a voice coach for, among others, Phyllis Hyman, Raquel Welch, and Jennifer Holiday.

"A good old girl of the kind folks call regular"

The irrepressible Ada Beatrice Queen Victoria Louisa Virginia Smith was born in what she called "West-by-God" Virginia in 1894 to a former slave and a barber. She took on the name Bricktop, in homage to her bright red hair, at the dawn of the Harlem Renaissance when she played at Barron's nightclub in New York, before moving to Europe. In 1924, she met Langston Hughes, then a starving artist, on her first night in Paris. Accustomed to playing big clubs, she literally cried when she saw the small size of Le Grand Duc, the club she was to play in the French capital. Hughes, a waiter at the club, assured her that most clubs in Montmartre were just as tiny. "Bricktop was simply a good old girl of the kind folks call regular," Hughes once said of his friend, who was able to attract demigods like Noël Coward, Pablo Picasso, Ernest Hemingway, and Cole Porter when she opened her first club in 1924. Even the Prince of Wales was a friend, and he hosted the opening night for one of her later clubs. Bricktop arrived in Paris just before Josephine Baker, at a time when black performers were still a bit of a novelty to club and theater audiences. Porter, who gave the down-to-earth redhead the idea to name her club "Bricktop's," asked her to teach him and his friends the Charleston. She was the inspiration behind one of the most famous songs by the great composer, "Miss Otis Regrets," after she relayed the story of man who was recently lynched in the South, ending with the line, "Well, that man won't lunch tomorrow."

VI/1

BRICKTOP

Her iconic Chez Bricktop nightclub in Paris was the playground for many expat Americans in the 1920s and '30s. It was also a starting point for many performers' careers. Among others, Bricktop (1894–1984) gave a start to the much lauded British-born singer Mabel Mercer (1900–1984), whom she took to New York with her on the outbreak of WWII. Bricktop continued to perform and entertain into her eighties. Photographed in 1939 by Carl Van Vechten.

VI/2

NORA HOLT

The multi-talented composer, musician and editor of her own publication, *Music and Poetry*, Holt (1885–1974) was also a frequent subject for gossip columnists of the 1920s and '30s. Photographed in 1932 by Carl Van Vechten.

VI/3

GLADYS BENTLEY

In the 1920s, Gladys (1907–1960) performed as "Bobbie Minton" and made her name as a male impersonator. Photographed here in 1932 by Carl Van Vechten, just as she was about to relocate to Los Angeles, she had lost weight and rejected her "mannish" style.

VI/4

ACQUANETTA

"She Fooled Hollywood." Born Mildred Davenport (1921–2004) in Norristown, Pennsylvania, photographed by Morgan and Marvin Smith holding a magazine with the ironic caption.

VI/5

EARTHA KITT

A move to Harlem with an aunt in the early 1940s led to the breaks that would allow her to leave poverty behind for good, but Eartha Kitt (1927–2008) experienced a different type of hardship, rejection, and backbreaking work throughout her six-decade-long career: endless hours of dance rehearsals and classes as both student and teacher; lessons to strengthen the distinctive, ambitious voice that alternately purred, seduced, and cajoled; the stress of putting her own money into film projects, like 1958's *Anna Lucasta*; and the strain of writing letters to Southern theater owners who refused to show the film purely on "racial grounds."

Kitt owned her sensuality in her music and on the stage and screen as she did in life, and it was displayed in her style choices: from the skin-tight mermaid gowns and smart, lady-like suits of the 1950s to the dramatic turbans, jewels, and animal prints of the 1960s and beyond. Kitt can't be reduced to a mere purr or come-hither wink, because there was always so much more—that unique blend of grit and elegance that makes her unforgettable to this day. Perhaps understandably, Kitt, who died of colon cancer in 2008, is best remembered for her role as Catwoman in the 1960s television version of *Batman*, quite an accomplishment given that she only appeared in three episodes. She also won an Emmy for playing a heroin-addicted nightclub singer in a memorable episode of *I Spy*. And, of course, there was *Boomerang*. Kitt also enjoyed an interesting movie career that went far beyond what are considered camp favorites today. In 1959 she starred opposite Sammy Davis, Jr. and a cast of greats from the black theater including Frederick O'Neal, the founder of the American Negro Theater, in the controversial (and watered down) film version of the hit all-black Broadway play, *Anna Lucasta*. Also in the cast were Rosetta LeNoire (best known as Mother Winslow from the television series *Family Matters*) and James Edwards, a fantastic unsung actor with leading man potential that sadly went unrealized.

This photograph, taken by Moneta Sleet, Jr. in 1956, shows Kitt next to a $650 mannequin that was said to be sculptured in her likeness. She was at the opening of Roxanne's Dressmaking Shop in New York City, which she co-owned. Later in her life, the international superstar would scorn makeup and take the utmost pleasure out of working in her garden, collecting birds' nests and relishing the feel of the earth beneath her manicured nails. "I'm a dirt person," she told *Ebony* in 1993. "I trust the dirt. I don't trust diamonds and gold."

VII

JAZZ SINGERS, MUSICIANS, & WRITERS

Billie Holiday, photographed in 1949 by Carl Van Vechten.

BILLIE HOLIDAY (1915–1959) is rarely thought of as someone who had many happy moments. She was best known for her troubled life and songs of anguished love ("Lover Man"), terror ("Strange Fruit"), and even suicide ("Gloomy Sunday"). Her dear friend Hazel Scott was among those who spoke up for her in a 1973 *Ebony* article defiantly titled "Lady Didn't Always Sing the Blues," published not long after the film *Lady Sings the Blues* was in theaters. "The thing I hope the kids don't miss—the ones who are just discovering Lady—is that she took a lot of the tragedy of her life and made something beautiful out of it; something very beautiful."

Just as ragtime had been attacked before it, when jazz gained momentum in the 1930s and 1940s, it was condemned far and wide by critics who were alarmed by the supposed moral decline the music would induce—especially considering the ostensible depravity of its roots in African-American music. Women in jazz, from singers to instrumentalists, had an additional hurdle to cross. Holiday began singing in small clubs in the 1930s where she was discovered by the white producer John Hammond. He put her in the recording studio right away, and she soon found herself singing in bigger and better-paying clubs. By the time she started singing with bandleaders Count Basie and Artie Shaw in the late 1930s, Lady had already enjoyed success with black listeners but was still largely unknown to wider audiences. That changed when she started playing the famed Greenwich Village club Café Society (Downtown), a place known for its stylish mixed-race crowd. Her problems with drugs and multiple arrests, however, eventually meant she needed to exert damage control over her image and career. She famously appeared on the cover of *Ebony* in 1949 with the headline "I'm Cured for Good." In an article that author Farah Jasmine Griffin called "a blatant bid for black middle class respectability" in her book *If You Can't Be Free, Be a Mystery: In Search of Billie Holiday*, the woman born Eleanora Fagan spoke directly to her readers in a first-person account that was most likely written by an editor. She gave glamorous and practical details of her newfound clean life. "I spent some $30,000 on new clothes, gowns, and a wonderful new fur coat. I bought a new Cadillac, sleek and pea green. I bought a little piece of land in Morristown, New Jersey, and started to build my dream house there." Sometime during her highs and lows of that year, Holiday found herself in Carl Van Vechten's studio to be photographed by him. As Griffin wrote in her book, "The photographer remembers photographing her for two hours, and while she was initially despondent, she returned from a brief sojourn 'on a different plane, all energy, sympathy, cooperation, and interest.' " A decade later, Holiday's drug and alcohol dependency would lead her to an all too early grave, just a month after her final arrest for narcotics possession. She had only $750 to her name.

Also in 1949, a former child prodigy named Nina Simone (1933–2003) was enjoying her first flush of fame, following the international success of her version of Gershwin's "I Loves You, Porgy." But not everything was plain sailing for the performer from then on.

A *Pittsburgh Courier* item that ran in 1965, for instance, told how just before being struck down with illness she had been tagged to make her movie debut in *Notorious Landlady* with Fred Astaire, Kim Novak, and Jack Lemmon. Simone was to sing two songs, including the title track, but she became ill with an ulcer. There were many articles with slightly startled tones about Simone for some time.

Born Eunice Kathleen Waymon in Tryon, North Carolina, she changed her name to Nina Simone ("Nina" meaning "little one" and "Simone" for the actress Simone Signoret) after she began singing in bars early in her career, something her Methodist minister mother,

Mary Kate Waymon, none too approvingly referred to as "working in the fires of hell." The prodigal Simone was playing piano by ear at three years old and was a regular pianist at her mother's church before she was ten. Her mother worked as a maid, and when her employer heard the young Simone play, she arranged for her to take piano lessons. Before long, the young girl had added Bach, Brahms, Chopin, and other classical composers to her repertoire. Although she received a grant to study at Juilliard, she applied to the Curtis Institute of Music in Philadelphia instead, and later said that she was denied admission based on race. By the early 1950s, she was playing piano in clubs under the name of Nina Simone, so that her mother wouldn't know. At the clubs, she blended blues and jazz and was soon a headliner. After signing with Bethlehem Records, a subsidiary of the influential (if Mafia-run) blues label King Records, Simone fought for the right to choose her own material and "I Loves You, Porgy"—her first hit—was the result. When she realized that she had unwittingly signed away the right to her royalties upon receiving her advance, she switched labels in 1959. She also changed the way she dressed and the way she wore her hair, as her consciousness was raised by the burgeoning civil rights movement in the United States. Simone was one of the first black public figures to proudly style her hair in an afro and wear elegant African-inspired designs onstage and off. This consciousness also found its way into her music, especially with protest songs like "Mississippi Goddam" and enduring personal compositions like "Four Women," a song that tells the story of four black women with four different complexions, four different hair textures, and four very different—and similar—stories of pain and struggle.

An adolescent star, Ella Fitzgerald (1917–1996) was discovered in 1934 when she won the famous Amateur Night contest at the Apollo Theater on Harlem's storied 125th Street. The win came after two years spent alternating between an orphanage and being homeless, following her mother's death in 1932. Although Fitzgerald wanted to be a dancer as a small child, singing proved to be a more useful occupation and her star began to rise in the swing era when she started singing with Chick Webb's band. She had her first big hit with a song that would become her signature tune, "A-tisket, A-tasket," in 1938. Remarkably, Fitzgerald took over Webb's band for three years after he died in 1939, at a time when there were few female leaders of predominantly male bands. Teaming up with Norman Granz's Jazz at the Philharmonic in 1946 brought her a large international following, and her legendary scatting—mimicking jazz instruments of the big bands—soon became one of the peerless elements of her act. She had even been known to imitate other singers like her friend Louis Armstrong, and Aretha Franklin. She was immediately influential at the peak of her career and that influence is still apparent today across genres from jazz and blues to world music.

Sarah Vaughan was yet another precocious child musician who was singing and playing the piano at church from a very early age. Born in Newark, New Jersey in 1924, she, like Fitzgerald, won the Apollo's Amateur Night competition (in 1942) and was soon singing and touring with big band leader Earl "Fatha" Hines. The next year, she would leave to work with her mentor, Billy Eckstine, who had seen her win that night at the Apollo. When Eckstine formed his own big band in 1944, Vaughan left her position as second pianist with Hines to join him and made her first recording with his orchestra on New Year's Eve of that year. She went out on her own in 1945 after a short stint as a soloist with another band leader named John Kirby. Her first husband, George Treadwell, was also her manager, and it was he who revamped her image on stage and helped her move into appearances on television and performing internationally. Soon, she was on stage with star jazz musicians like Dizzy Gillespie and she recorded a gorgeous version of "Lover Man" with Charlie Parker in 1945.

Vaughn spent the first five years of the 1950s with Columbia Records, recording mostly with its in-house orchestras, with the exception of a jazz recording with Miles Davis in 1950. In 1982, she won her first Grammy Award for her album of Gershwin tunes, *Gershwin Live*. After a career of many accolades, including an Emmy Award for individual achievement in 1981 and a Grammy Award for lifetime achievement in 1989, she continued to record and perform until her health failed and she died of lung cancer at the age of 66 on April 4, 1990.

Nancy Wilson (b. 1937) was clear on her goals as a singer when she arrived in New York City in 1959. The Ohioan already had an idea of her place on the food chain and took comparisons to icons in her stride.

> Dinah Washington had a great deal of humor. If I were to describe myself, I'd say there's a lot of Dinah—Dinah's humor. I don't sound that much like Dinah although people compared me to her. I think that the chit-chat, the general humor, is a lot of Dinah. The overall look would be Lena Horne. The sound is Jimmy Scott. So it's a combination of things and the bottom line: by osmosis. I became me from listening, absorbing things from everybody.

Wilson had done her homework and knew exactly what she wanted. "I wanted to have John Levy manage me and Dave Cavanaugh produce me at Capitol Records. That was my plan, and I got it all in five weeks!" she said in a 2004 interview.

> I knew that John was a decent human being. I'd heard nothing but good things about him and knew that he would understand what I wanted to do. I wanted to be a cross between Lena Horne and Dinah Washington and play the good rooms. I didn't want to be playing in sawdust. I thought it might be a great crossover opportunity for John, allowing him to get out of the strictly jazz field, and it was a great chance for me to have a manager who gave a damn.

She would later say, "I think the problem is that most people don't go with an agenda. The idea, to me, if you go, is to have some names and to know where you're going as opposed to [just arrive in] New York and think you can stand on a corner and sing and somebody's going to hear you. It doesn't work that way. You need something specific. You need to know... what your objective is." Wilson enjoyed a long and illustrious career that included pop singles (particularly the Grammy-winning "[You Don't Know How] Glad I Am" in 1963, jazz and R&B albums, and two more Grammy-winning albums in 2004 and 2006. She was a prominent participator in numerous civil rights marches in the 1960s, and in 2005 was inducted into the International Civil Rights Walk of Fame at the Martin Luther King Historic site in Atlanta, Georgia.

VII/1

ELLA FITZGERALD

Performing in a Chicago nightclub in 1958. "I know I'm no glamour girl," Ella (1917–1996) once remarked, "and it's not easy for me to get up in front of a crowd of people. It used to bother me a lot, but now I've got it figured out that God gave me this talent to use, so I just stand there and sing."

VII/2

SARAH VAUGHAN

Photographed in London in 1960. Even as she sang during the last years of her life (1924–1990), her glorious voice never lost an ounce of its luster.

VII/3

DINAH WASHINGTON

Best known today for her rendition of "Mad About the Boy" following its use in a 1992 Levi's ad, Alabama-born Ruth Lee Jones (1924–1963) was one of the most successful female singers of the 1950s. As Dinah Washington, she scored a string of R&B hits between 1948 and 1963, while at the same time earning a reputation as one of the best jazz vocalists around for her work with, among others, Cannonball Adderley, Clark Terry, and Ben Webster.

VII/4

SHIRLEY BASSEY

The Welsh singer (b. 1937) being prepared for performance in 1960.

VII/5

MIRIAM MAKEBA

The legendary South African singer and civil rights activist (1932–2008), photographed in 1960.

VII/6

CELIA CRUZ

"The Queen of Salsa" (1925–2003), shown as a young singer in the 1950s. Born in Havana, Cuba, she gained fame as the lead singer of La Sonora Mantancera, a popular Cuban orchestra. Her famous catch phrase, "*Azucar!*" was said to be an allusion to African slaves who worked Cuba's sugar plantations.

To Louie
Sincerely
Blanche Calloway
Mauricé
CHICAGO

BLANCHE CALLOWAY

Women instrumentalists are rarely in the spotlight the way singers are, but they have been around, in jazz, bebop, and classical, from the beginning. While there have been many outstanding women players, from saxophonists and trumpeters to all-women jazz bands like the International Sweethearts of Rhythm, only a few have received their rightful due. All-girl bands started gaining momentum in the 1930s and a large number of them were African-American. Popular groups like the Harlem Playgirls were not able to play to the same lucrative venues as white all-girl bands, but they did gain a foothold in the industry until the mid-1940s, when male musicians began to return home from World War II to take back their old jobs or form new bands.

There were not many women leading men in any capacity at the time, but Blanche Calloway, older sister to bandleader Cab Calloway, was the first of them. She was a chorus girl on the black vaudeville circuit with the Smarter Set Co. early in her career, one of the dancing chorus girls called "World Famous Bronze Beauties." She was plucked out of the lineup to act in sketches and toured with several cabarets before venturing out as a singer and earning high praise from stars of the day. like the pianist Earl Hines. He would later write, "Blanche Calloway... had a very good way of entertaining. She was wild and wiry in certain things, and very sensitive when it came to balance."

She was born Blanche Dorothea Jones Calloway in Rochester, New York on February 9, 1902. Her mother, Martha Eulalia, was a music teacher and her father, Cabell, was an attorney, who died when she was eight (her mother remarried, to an insurance salesman). Martha encouraged her musical talents but also valued education very highly and was not pleased when the young woman dropped out of Morgan College to pursue a career in entertainment. In 1921, Calloway joined the cast of *Shuffle Along* when it toured the country after its successful Broadway run, and two years later joined the cast of *Plantation Days*, one of the most famous African-American touring revues of that decade. In November 1925, she was living in Chicago headlining at "Chicago's Classiest Cabaret," the Sunset Café, when she made her first record for the Okeh label with her new group, Blanche Calloway and her Joy Boys—one of whom was Louis Armstrong, making some of his earliest recordings. The Chicago show seems to have been a smaller version of the full stage revue, designed to run in a nightclub called the Plantation Café. A November 17, 1925 article in the *Chicago Defender* tells of the Plantation Café's downturn:

"This black and tan resort in the heart of the colored [district] once catered to a vast number of whites... It has recently become inhabited with undesirable characters whose actions have driven off practically all the white trade. White people are now given no protection when entering... four white couples and approximately twenty colored people were present when this reviewer witnessed this 'Plantation Revue.' The show is presented in sections... The Five Crackerjacks are the feature... Blanche Calloway, good prima donna, but also misplaced..."

Calloway left the revue to move in with Henry Waddy, who would eventually become her agent, manager, and common-law husband. Waddy, who was as fond of flashy living as Calloway's baby brother, Cab, moved to New York with Blanche, where she spent the early part of 1926 performing at Ciro's nightclub. When a full-scale revival of *Plantation Days* was staged, with a planned national tour kicking off in Chicago later that fall, Blanche once again joined the cast. Alyn Shipton writes in his book, *Hi-De-Ho: The Life of Cab Calloway*, that Blanche and Cab Calloway performed together several times, including in a notable revue in June 1927 that featured an up-and-coming singer named Adelaide Hall. Calloway influence on the early part of her brother's career was undeniable. According to Earl Hines, Calloway came to him and Louis Armstrong at the Sunset Café one day and appealed to them to hire her brother. According to Shipton, Calloway family legend had Blanche Calloway in a brief romance with Armstrong at the time, even though she was still with Waddy. Cab was hired at the Sunset at $35 a week—compare that to his sister's $200 a week—but his star began to rise soon after. After her music career ended, Calloway had a significant career in real estate and was the programming director for a radio station in Florida for many years.

In 1968, Calloway founded AFRAM House, a mail-order company that made cosmetics and toiletries for black consumers. "Quite frankly," she told the *New York Times* in 1969, "we got tired of buying white products and trying to adapt them to our needs. Black or white, everyone wants to look attractive. But, we blacks just can't expect results from cosmetics designed for white skins." The company's name was an acronym for African-American and it was successful right away, selling at major stores like J.C. Penney; Sears, Roebuck; and Montgomery Ward. AFRAM's colorful mail-order catalogues featured cosmetics, wigs, jewelry, sunglasses, African art objects, and a line of Soul Brother toiletries. Advertisements with coupons were placed in black publications and orders poured in from around the country. "I didn't doubt for a minute that we would be successful," she continued in the *Times*. "Years ago, there was no need for the black woman to develop a consciousness of cosmetics. Let's face it; she just didn't need cosmetics then. Her job outside the home was a maid or housekeeper. She didn't need to look attractive. And she couldn't afford to, anyway."

VII/8

OLIVETTE MILLER

The celebrated swing harpist, circa 1940s. Miller (1914–2003), was the daughter of Bessie Oliver, a 1900s chorus girl, and Flournoy Miller, the venerable actor, comedian, writer, and producer, who co-wrote and produced the groundbreaking Broadway musical *Shuffle Along*. Raised on Harlem's famous Striver's Row, she graduated from East Greenwich Academy, a private Methodist boarding school in Rhode Island, in 1931 and studied music in Paris and at Juilliard School in New York City. Miller's stunning beauty and colorful love-life kept her in the newspapers almost as much as her music. She performed with both Lena Horne and a young Dorothy Dandridge in the 1940s; played at top-notch night clubs in Hollywood, Chicago, and New York; and made a few appearances on *The Ed Sullivan Show* in the 1960s.

VII/9

VALAIDA SNOW

A renowned musician and composer (1904–1956), conducting an orchestra in London in October 1934.

MARY LOU WILLIAMS

Mary Lou Williams (1910–1981), circa 1944. Williams began performing professionally while still a child. Born in Atlanta in 1910 and raised in Pittsburgh, she used her stepfather's name, performing as Mary Lou Burley until, not yet an adult, she met and married John Williams in 1925 after joining his band. She was the primary composer and arranger for the outfit even after her husband left on Andy Kirk's arrival as leader. Critics acknowledge that the surge in popularity enjoyed by the band was due to her distinctive arrangements, compositions, and solo performances on piano. She was also called on to write scores for leaders in the field like Benny Goodman, Earl Hines, and Tommy Dorsey. Williams was one the few female musicians to get respect and recognition on a par with her male peers, and her apartment on Hamilton Terrace in Harlem often served as a salon where the best jazz musicians could eat and talk late into the night. Her performances with her husband's band helped it become a major influence on the Kansas City big band sound. She later worked with bebop musicians including Thelonious Monk and founded her own record label. Williams died of bladder cancer in 1981 in Durham, North, Carolina, when she was Artist in Residence at Duke University.

VII/11

HAZEL SCOTT

Performing, with Paul Robeson in the background, at a dinner in Brooklyn in honor of Hugh Mulzac, the first African-American captain in the U.S. Navy to command an integrated crew during World War II. Born in Trinidad, Scott (1920–1981) had her hands insured by Lloyd's of London and was known to have a special place in her heart for diamonds from Harry Winston. Onc critic noted that Scott "knows and can play the classics... but she knows how to swing them." Swinging the classics became a trademark for her, coupled with her glamorous and versatile presentation and performances, and she made appearances on the silver screen and was the first black woman to host her own television show.

VII/12

LOIS TOWLES

Dorothea's older sister, seen here in fur with luggage on the way to Europe. A *magna cum laude* graduate of Wiley College in Marshall, Texas, Towles (1912–1983) also earned two master's degrees from the University of Iowa. She was working on a doctoral degree in music from Juilliard School in New York when her career really took off. In early 1950, Towles returned to the United States for a 30-day concert tour to the country's major cities and colleges, including her New York debut at the Town Hall, before resuming her professorship at Fisk.

VII/13

ZORA NEALE HURSTON

In an article written in 1950 titled, "What White Publishers Won't Print", writer and anthropologist Hurston (1891–1961), seen here in a photo taken in Chicago in 1934 by Carl Van Vechten, stated that, "For various reasons, the average, struggling, non-morbid Negro is the best-kept secret in America. His revelation to the public is the thing needed to do away with that feeling of difference which inspires fear, and which ever expresses itself in dislike. It is inevitable that this knowledge will destroy many illusions and romantic traditions which America probably likes to have around. But then, we have no record of anybody sinking into a lingering death on finding out that there was no Santa Claus. The old world will take it in its stride. The realization that Negroes are no better nor no worse, and at times just as bonny as everybody else, will hardly kill off the population of the nation."

VII/14

LADY BIRD CLEVELAND

"I was a fly chick when I was young." So the fine artist (b. 1926, now Lady Bird Strickland) described herself to a reporter in 2012 in a story about an exhibition of her paintings. Strickland, the mother of legendary fashion model Pat Cleveland, painted portraits of Harlem musicians and club scenes in the 1950s. She met and married a Swedish sax player, gave birth to Pat and virtually raised her single handed after the marriage split. Photographed here by Carl Van Vechten on September 21, 1954.

VII/15

BARBARA MCNAIR

A singer and actor, McNair (1934–2007) starred on Broadway, had hit records and was the first African-American woman to host her own variety show on television from 1969 to 1971.

LORRAINE HANSBERRY

The author and playwright (1930–1965) inspired Nina Simone to write "To Be Young, Gifted And Black" in 1970. She was also the godmother of Simone's daughter. She first found fame in 1959 when her play *A Raisin in the Sun* became a Broadway hit. Born in Chicago she moved to Harlem in 1951, where she joined W.E.B. Du Bois on the *Freedom* newspaper. An outspoken civil rights activist, she also wrote articles promoting gay rights and feminist thought. *A Raisin in the Sun* made her the first black female playwright to be produced on Broadway and the fifth woman to receive the New York Drama Critics Circle Award for Best New Drama. Following her tragic death from cancer, James Baldwin said, "It is not at all far fetched to suspect that what she saw contributed to the strain which killed her, for the effort to which Lorraine was dedicated is more than enough to kill a man."

VII/17

MAYA ANGELOU

The renowned writer (1928–2014) was a nightclub singer and a dancer on Broadway before she became better known as a poet and a bestselling author. She has also written screenplays for films such as 1972's *Georgia, Georgia*, starring Diana Sands, and directed the 1982 television movie, *Sister, Sister*, which starred Diahann Carroll, Rosalind Cash, and Irene Cara.

MOVIE STARS, THEATER, & TV PIONEERS

Rosalind Cash (1938–1995) in a scene from the film *Melinda*, 1972.

Diahann Carroll (b. 1935) was careful to explain why she was so astonished at the sight of Diana Ross, her "huge head of hair flying in the wind," sailing through Beverly Hills in a bright yellow Bentley convertible one day in 1976. As she explained in her 2008 memoir, *The Legs Are the Last to Go*, although the music industry, and the world, had been impacted by the power of Motown for more than a decade, Carroll was having trouble adjusting when it came to her own career. "I knew it was brilliant," she wrote, "but I simply couldn't relate to it. I was immersed in an old-fashioned notion of elegance and sophistication and had no choice but to remain true to the music of Gershwin, Porter, and Ellington—what I knew and was raised on. All this new music represented a loss of footing for me."

By the 1970s, bona fide Oscar-nominated stars like Carroll and Ross still found that quality film roles were few and far between, even for established black actresses. "They wanted me to play the girlfriend," said Nichelle Nichols (b. 1932) to the *Wall Street Journal* in 2011 of her role in the 1974 film, *Truck Turner*, which featured Isaac Hayes in his first and only starring role. "All you saw in blaxploitation films was the Aunt Jemima, flirty girl, or the hooker. I said, I'll play the madam and she'll be so fantastic. The producers told me the madam was supposed to be this 350-pound black woman. I said no, that's just what's on the paper. What if she was tough, no-nonsense, and mean because of the life she'd lived, but elegant as well?"

It is easy to see why Nichols would be so hopeful. Less than a decade earlier, she made television history in her role as Lieutenant Uhura on *Star Trek* (1966–69) by becoming the first black woman to be cast in a regular role on the small screen. The idea of television stardom was still relatively new at the time and Nichols was not immediately aware of the impact of her appearance on the show, especially for a black audience that was so unaccustomed to seeing black faces on television. Thinking she would go back to her Broadway roots, and dissatisfied with changes on set at the show, Nichols nearly left after the first season, but a chance meeting with Dr. Martin Luther King, Jr. at a fundraiser changed her mind. After King told her that he was her "greatest fan," she thanked him and informed him of her decision to leave the show. "He asked what I was talking about, and told me that I can't leave the show. We talked a long time about what it all meant and what images on television tell us about ourselves," Nichols said in a 2011 interview with the *Wall Street Journal*'s Speakeasy blog.

Donald Bogle said of the actress Rosalind Cash (1938–1995) in his book, *Brown Sugar: Over 100 Years of America's Black Female Superstars* (2007), "Seldom in Hollywood's history was a black woman so repeatedly wasted, so thoroughly trashed by the industry. And the roles this gifted woman found herself playing often revealed Hollywood's basic contempt for the talented, not-easily-typed black actress. In a way, though, the roles, coupled with Cash's high-strung artistry, created a persona for her. As with Gloria Foster, perceptive audiences sat watching Rosalind Cash, using her as a symbol of their own broken promises and unfulfilled dreams." Early in her career, Cash was Barbara McNair's understudy on Broadway in *No Strings*. In an interview with Bogle in the *New York Times* in 1973, long before he made that observation, Cash offered an interesting take on some of the actresses who came before her, including Dorothy Dandridge.

> I remember having a love-hate thing for Dorothy Dandridge. As scrawny, ashamed little black kids, we would make fun of her, assuming she couldn't act because she

> really didn't reflect our mothers or our aunts. Later on, I saw her again and thought she was one of the finest film actresses I've ever seen in my life. But I didn't appreciate that until much later because, well, I came from the streets and I didn't know anyone who acted like her. I knew some bourgeois people on the other side of town who tried to act like Dorothy Dandridge, but they didn't succeed because it was Atlantic City, N.J. and no one was that pretty.

Cash was openly critical of Hollywood for "trying to force" her into "tragic mulatto" roles based on her looks. "Hollywood felt that I would fit right into that pattern, but my soul was against it."

Ellen Holly (b. 1931) expressed her discontentment with the limitations imposed on black actresses in a spate of articles that appeared in the *New York Times* in the late 1960s and early '70s. In one article, she wrote about a screenplay that she had researched and written, inspired by the life of Henri Christophe, the 18th-century Haitian revolution leader. She envisioned a film, "projected in my imagination, finished, produced by a mythological black film company emotionally equipped to enter into the obsession, performed by a dream cast inspired by its own history: Calvin Lockhart as the central male character, Roscoe Lee Browne as his uncle, and the Senagalese actor, Badou, as Henri Christophe. At first the projection was hazy, but gradually it got so clear that I knew the composition of almost every shot, could even itemize objects on tables."

But alas, her dream was not to be—which hardly surprised her. She shopped the script to Hollywood studios to no avail. Interesting, nuanced work that explored previously untapped aspects of history, and that happened to provide meaty, dignified roles for black actors, was rare to nonexistent. Susan Fales-Hill's memoir about her mother, Josephine Premice (1926–2001), *Always Wear Joy*, tells the story of her mother's exasperation at being told by a producer that she didn't look maternal enough for a role. "I have two children, no dishwasher, and a dog. Is that maternal enough for you?" Fales-Hill observed that performing gave her mother "a chance to express something deep within her, something no amount of cooking, bargain hunting, and home decorating could ever satisfy." For years, Premice and her friends would talk about the magical time they were able to perform *A Hand Is on the Gate* (1966) on Broadway and sing and recite the work of Langston Hughes, Gwendolyn Brooks, Paul Lawrence Dunbar, and other poets and songwriters.

A notable exception in this dearth of quality black roles came courtesy of the Negro Ensemble Company, formed in 1968. Many of the top actresses of the 1960s and '70s were veterans of the Negro Ensemble Company, including several women recognizable from their roles in long-running television sitcoms. Among them was Esther Rolle, best known for her portrayal of the matriarch in the television series *Good Times*, who had been dancing professionally for more than a decade by the time she joined the Negro Ensemble Company. Roxie Roker was another, a Howard University graduate who was nominated for a Tony Award for her role in *The River Niger*, as was Hattie Winston, the first black person to appear in a nationally televised commercial. Winston would go on to appear on the PBS children's series *The Electric Company* and enjoy extensive television and voice-over work, including the voice of Lucy Carmichael in *The Rugrats Movie*. Actresses like Phylicia Rashad, Angela Bassett, Mary Alice, Clarice Taylor, Lynn Whitfield, and S. Epatha Merkerson also came through the landmark theater company.

Diana Sands (1934–1973)—best known for her fiery portrayal of Beneatha Younger, the clever, quick-tempered kid sister of Sidney Poitier's Walter Lee Younger in both the 1959 stage and 1961 film versions of Lorraine Hansberry's *A Raisin in the Sun*—lamented in the *New York Times*, "The Negro female has been categorized as a neuter, a mammy, and an exotic. Why isn't she a mother, a wife, a woman, a desirable object, a woman desired and feminine, someone who embodies all the characteristics of American womanhood? Did you know that 30 percent of the movie audience is Negro? Maybe the moviemakers don't like Negroes on principle. Maybe they will like money. I would like the freedom to play roles people think I'm right for—and not based on color. I want that for everybody. When I started out, there was no place to train. Not only to be denied opportunity but to be denied opportunity to learn—that is to be stunted at the root."

Sands, a native of the Bronx and graduate of New York City's fabled School of Performing Arts, worked as a dancer and carnival singer to support herself early in her career. Later she was nominated for Tony Awards for her performances in *The Owl and the Pussycat* and James Baldwin's *Blues for Mister Charlie* in 1964. Even though Sands earned constant critical praise, quality roles rarely materialized for her. She often spoke out about the stereotypical characters that black actresses were relegated to playing. "Most white actresses who have been received as I have been received on Broadway and television wouldn't have to go into repertory theater. They wouldn't have the time," she lamented in a 1968 *Look* magazine interview. She had been thrilled about starring on Broadway in *The Owl and the Pussycat* with Alan Alda in 1965. And for good reason, as she said at the time, "This is the first Broadway play in which I was cast as a person, rather than a racial type. I love doing it. When it's over, the owl and the pussycat leave hand in hand to dance by the light of the moon."

But, as she told *Look* magazine, "The way the setup is, I had no choice but to go to repertory if I wanted to do roles that offer me some kind of challenge, besides racial roles. Because I have other things to say. Race is not the only problem I have. I have all the problems of woman, of a person, of a citizen. I know certain things about life that have nothing to do with color, things I want to express. Name me a movie where a black woman has been loved and treated as a woman, you know—as a woman, a woman—someone to bear your children, someone whom you would protect, someone whom you would love gently. It's not allowed. You never see it."

Her uneven film career had moments of brilliance, though. She earned rave reviews for her portrayals of a remorseful, adulterous wife in the 1970 film *The Landlord* and a complex superstar singer who falls for a white U.S. Army defector in *Georgia, Georgia* (1972), written by Maya Angelou. Sadly her bright light burned out fast, and at only 39 Sands succumbed to cancer, just a month before her wedding. Prior to her illness, she was cast as the lead in *Claudine* (1974). Too sick to play the part, Sands insisted it go to her friend, Diahann Carroll, who had seen to it that Sands had a recurring role on her 1960s groundbreaking TV hit, *Julia*.

VIII/1

PEARL BAILEY

The singer (1918–1990) photographed by Carl Van Vechten in 1946. Bailey earned a B.A. in theology from Georgetown University in 1985 at the age of 67. Initially, she majored in French but switched to theology, "because it's easier to know the Lord than it is to know French."

VIII/2

NICHELLE NICHOLS

The actress was a jazz singer (b. 1932) before she made her mark as Lieutenant Uhura on *Star Trek* in 1966.

VIII/3

CICELY TYSON

The actor (b. 1933) on the red carpet at the Oscars ceremony on March 27, 1973. She was nominated for Best Actress for her role in *Sounder* (1972).

VIII/4

DENISE NICHOLAS

Photographed in September 1969. Best known as school counselor Liz McIntyre from the groundbreaking television show *Room 222*, Nicholas (b. 1944) also starred in—and wrote for—the drama *In the Heat of the Night* in the 1980s. In 2005, she released her debut novel *Freshwater Road*, which was loosely based on her own life. The novel follows a young Michigan woman's journey south as a volunteer during 1964's Freedom Summer.

VIII/5

DIANA SANDS

The outspoken and hugely talented actor, (1934–1973) photographed in 1962 by Carl Van Vechten.

VIII/6

TERESA GRAVES

The first black woman to star in her own long-running TV drama series, *Jet* magazine called her "television's most delightful detective" for her portrayal of Christie Love in the series of the same name. A Texan, Graves (1948–2002) was a singer and actress who came to prominence in *Rowan and Martin's Laugh-In* in 1970. Her comedic talents landed her the lead in *Vampira* (1974), directed by Clive Donner and co-starring David Niven. She became a Jehovah's Witness, campaigned against her religion's persecution in Malawi, and retired in 1983 to care for her mother.

VIII/7

DIAHANN CARROLL

In 1960, *New York Times* music critic John S. Wilson observed that Diahann Carroll was "very reminiscent of Miss Horne." It was an observation no one would have made just five years earlier. Thanks in part to composer and arranger Phil Moore's cultivation, Carroll was already morphing from a sweet, wide-eyed ingénue to the glamorous diva she would be known as for the rest of her career. Just a few years before her Tony-nominated debut in Truman Capote's *House of Flowers*, Carroll was ready—under Moore's watchful eye—to blossom. Wilson called her *The Persian Room Presents Diahann Carroll* performance "a vivid demonstration that Miss Carroll had developed a very slick, highly mannered presentation, craftily paced, skillfully executed, and polished to a magnificent sheen."

Carroll happened to be the first black performer to sit on the coveted *Tonight Show* couch when the show was hosted by Jack Paar. He acknowledged this fact in his memoir, *P.S. Jack Paar: An Entertainment* (1983) and wrote, "I suddenly realized that in our year or more on *The Tonight Show*, while there were black performers on, I had not actually sat down with one and talked. This may seem a strange thing to say now, but I do it only in the historical context. It just had not been done on any program or panel show that I knew of." She appeared on the show more than a dozen times, and it was where Richard Rodgers spotted her for the first time and felt compelled to call her the next day with an unforgettable opportunity.

"He said that he would like to do a musical with me and that he'd like me to be as he saw me on the television show," Carroll wrote in *The Legs Are the Last to Go*. "The day that he asked me to join him for lunch before he left for Europe, I thought it was very important that I startle him when I arrived at the restaurant. I think that business of overwhelming people with your presence, and your grooming—it's not a part of today. It's not important today. I cannot tell you what it meant then. I was dressed in Givenchy from head to toe. It meant a great deal during an interview."

Not overtly political, she nevertheless tried to get a positive message across in the work she chose to do. She told *Ebony* in a 1962 cover story, "*No Strings* is no message show. It is wonderful entertainment with beautiful music, but it does something that I feel has never been done on the Broadway stage: it glorifies the American Negro woman as she has never been glorified before by the theater in this country. Until now, roles like that of Barbara Woodruff, the character I play, were monopolized by white actresses. I am proud to play Barbara Woodruff, a Negro girl of sophistication and taste. There are many real-life Barbara Woodruffs all over America awaiting the chance to do the things she does in *No Strings*."

As her groundbreaking television show, *Julia*, made its debut, Carroll refused to sit through interviews without her publicist by her side and she insisted that all "racial quotes" be read back to her. Judy Stone of the *New York Times* explained to readers that Ms. Carroll had impressed upon her that "there are nuances that escape even the most well-meaning white reporters" and, after one particularly troubling story, stipulations were put in place for further interviews. Describing one such well-meaning reporter, Carroll said, "He was not aware that a little word here and a little word there could kill me. I told him I think everything going on in the black community now has a more positive feeling than before. He wanted me to say that a certain element was detrimental and I wouldn't." Even after she was nominated for an Academy Award for *Claudine*, Carroll told *Ebony* in 1975, "I'm afraid the amount of money I've made in motion pictures in the last fifteen years wouldn't afford the rent on this room," referring to the den in her Los Angeles home. "I'm very happy that I can eat by singing a song. I have come a long way on being half-cute and working in nightclubs. I want something to challenge me to push myself as far as I can go emotionally."

SOUL SISTERS, PERFECT ANGELS, & ROCK-AND-ROLL DIVAS

KOOL

Aretha Franklin (b. 1942) in her dressing room at Newark Symphony Hall in 1969.

When Maxine Powell (1915–2013) opened the Motown Finishing School in 1964, she started out with two simple questions for the artists that she was cultivating: *Who are you? What makes you tick?* Esther Gordy Edwards and Gwen Gordy, two sisters of Motown founder Berry Gordy, soon urged their brother to bring the owner of the Maxine Powell Finishing and Modeling School to his growing record label to help polish his artists. Powell, herself a former student at the Madam C.J. Walker School of Beauty Culture, taught etiquette to male and female acts alike, from the Temptations to the Supremes. This included how to get in and out of cars, how to use props on stage, and the proper way to greet important guests who visited backstage after a show. "We worked with developing class. I helped them to eliminate shyness and get rid of any hang-ups because oftentimes we start with body language, your body language tells so much about you, don't even have to say a word." The graceful elegance of the Supremes would inspire for generations, in and out of the music business. The sight of Diana Ross, Mary Wilson, and Florence Ballard always looking beautiful and handling themselves so well on nationwide television programs like the *Ed Sullivan Show*, and in pictures from around the world, enthralled fans of all races and were a source of special pride to many American black women.

An early review in a 1968 issue of *Vogue* raved about a "coiffed and spangled" Aretha Franklin singing "three gratuitous hits to warm up," and then proceeding to sit down at her piano and "usher in the spirit of ecstasy." It was an apt description of the woman who was emerging out of the church and a conservative early career singing the blues and jazz *à la* Dinah Washington. Refashioned as a pop singer when she made the switch from Columbia to Atlantic Records in the late '60s, Franklin took the opportunity to begin experimenting with her wardrobe choices right along with her music—after which she never looked back. As she soared in popularity, she was rhapsodized in "Poem for Aretha" (1970) by Nikki Giovanni:

she is undoubtedly the one person who put everyone on notice
she revived johnny ace and remembered lil green aretha sings
"I say a little prayer" and dionne doesn't
want to hear it anymore
aretha sings "money won't change you"
but james can't sing "respect" the advent
of Aretha pulled ray charles from marlboro country
and back into
the blues made nancy wilson
try one more time forced
dionne to make a choice (she opted for the movies)
and diana ross had to get an afro wig pushed every
Black singer into Blackness and negro entertainers
into negroness you couldn't jive
when she said you make me feel

If Aretha's music gave voice to the everyday "do right" black woman, her style choices showed you what she looked like when she dressed up: Afros, sometimes dyed red, to match flowing, custom-made gowns from black designers like Stephen Burrows. An all-natural look without makeup, worn with a hand-sewn dashiki. Or a sleek press-and-curl to complement

Minnie Riperton (1947–1979) photographed in 1975.

glittering, beaded, low-cut stage gowns, like the one she wore in a 1970s advertisement for Fashion Fair cosmetics. Even when she went "too far" by the standards of others, she ultimately seemed pretty pleased with herself.

As the natural came into style in the 1970s in hair, makeup, and outlook, fresh-faced beauties who could be called songbirds without a trace of irony came to the fore. Witness Chaka Khan's feather earrings, or the baby's breath in Minnie Riperton's hair and the ice cream cone dripping down her hand on the cover of *Perfect Angel* (1974). Suddenly, black women were allowed to let their hair down again. Deniece Williams, formerly a part of Wonderlove (background vocalists for Stevie Wonder), had a hit with her song "Free" (1976). Natalie Cole was doing well in the family business with a string of hits that included "Inseparable" (1975), "This Will Be" (1975), and "Our Love" (1977).

Riperton (1947–1979) told a reporter in 1974 that Stevie Wonder wrote the song "Perfect Angel" for her and about her because he felt that the song was an expression of her spirit. "That's what he thinks I am. It is really a nice gift." In a way, the Chicago-born Riperton was archetypal of a certain type of black female singer that rose to prominence in the 1970s: feminine, charming, soft-spoken women who embodied a "girl next door" that was more familiar to a black audience than the typically blond, blue-eyed embodiment usually touted in the media. Riperton started her career as a teenager in a group called the Gems who recorded on Chess Records and sang background for just about every major act on the label, including Etta James, Muddy Waters, and Bo Diddley. After a brief period with the Rotary Connection, she went solo. An accomplished songwriter, she often teamed with her husband, Richard Rudolph, and they wrote her signature tune, "Lovin' You" (1975). "Sometimes I write the melodies and he writes the lyrics," she explained in a 1974 interview; "sometimes he writes the melodies and I write the lyrics. The songs we write and I do are about my life, really. That is what I have been doing, raising my family and writing. I'm not crazy about making money, but I enjoy life." She also enjoyed fashion and eagerly talked in detail to one reporter about the clothes she was wearing (a silk organza blouse and long brown velvet skirt). "It was designed by Ola Hudson, a Libra lady. We get along just fine. Have the same taste in food and clothes. Ola designs to the person. She did all the Pointers Sister things just about." Hudson, who was black, also designed costumes for music legends David Bowie, John Lennon, and Diana Ross. She was better known in later years as the mother of the guitarist Saul "Slash" Hudson of the rock band Guns N' Roses.

A year after being diagnosed with cancer and having a mastectomy at the age of just 28, Riperton told the *New York Times*, "I wanted to tell people about it." However, initially she kept mum on her diagnosis and no one knew about her illness except close friends like Stevie Wonder. "It had nothing to do with publicity. I wanted to tell people it could happen to me, a young woman. And that women don't have to live in fear with their lovers or their husbands or whatever. It doesn't have to ruin you sexually. Is that what they love you for—your breasts? Life is so much more than that. We should be in touch with ourselves, to realize that our bodies are working for us and not against us."

She was a brave and responsible person who, like many of her peer group, used her position as a well-known artist to spread the right kind of message about what it meant to be a woman and to be a black woman, in times that were more than difficult for them. It was the example of Riperton and the other great singers and performers of the seventies who made it easier for the artists who followed, from Anita Baker to Jill Scott.

IX/1

GLADYS KNIGHT

The Atlanta-born singer (b. 1944) fronted a band of family members from the age of 8. After success with Motown Records in the late 1960s, Gladys Knight and the Pips were a staple of pop charts around the world until 1988, when they disbanded. Her subsequent solo career has resulted in numerous hits and 4 Grammy Awards.

IX/2

DIONNE WARWICK

The internationally famous singer, actor and TV host was born in East Orange, New Jersey in 1940. In her 70s she became a UN Global Ambassador for food and agriculture. She is one of the most successful pop singers of all time.

IX/3

THE SUPREMES

L–R: Mary Wilson (b. 1944), Florence Ballard (1943–1976), and Diana Ross (b. 1944) arrive in London at Heathrow Airport in 1964.

IX/4

LABELLE

L–R: Patti LaBelle (b. 1944), Sarah Dash (b. 1945), and Nona Hendryx (b. 1944) in the 1970s. They were first known as the Bluebelles, a doo-wop group in the early 1960s, and then as Patti LaBelle and the Bluebelles, before scoring their biggest hit with "Lady Marmalade" in 1974 as LaBelle.

IX/5

THE POINTER SISTERS

L–R: June (1953–2006), Ruth (b. 1946), Bonnie (b. 1950), and Anita (b. 1948) wearing 1940s vintage styles in 1973. The sisters were preacher's daughters who topped the R&B and pop charts and were nominated for over a dozen Grammy Awards in the pop, R&B, and country categories. They were also the first black female group to sing at the Grand Ole Opry.

IX/6

NATALIE COLE

The oldest daughter of Nat "King" Cole and Maria Cole, by her mid-20s Natalie (b. 1950) was a disco-singing superstar, most famous for the Grammy Award-winning "This Will Be" (1975). In 1992, she swept all six categories she was nominated in at the Grammy Awards for her 1991 album, *Unforgettable*, which featured a technology-assisted duet with her late father.

IX/7

BETTY DAVIS

Rock and funk trailblazer Betty Davis (b. 1945) in February 1976. A model for magazines like *Ebony*, *Seventeen*, and *Glamour* as a teenager, she married Miles Davis in 1968. She introduced Miles to the music of her friends Jimi Hendrix and Sly Stone, but her own musical career was tumultuous. She wrote all of her own songs and even wrote for bands like the Commodores, but her brash, sexual stage persona and lyrics drew protests from groups like the NAACP and resistance from record labels who wanted her to be more commercial. Refusing to compromise, she backed away from the music business in the early 1980s. In 2009, Light tn the Attic Records released some of her long-lost albums.

IX/8

A TASTE OF HONEY

Janice Marie Johnson (b. 1954, bass), left, and Hazel Payne (b. 1956, guitar) were best known for the 1978 album *A Taste of Honey*, which contained their biggest hit, "Boogie Oogie Oogie." As the story about the song goes, they were onstage at a military base and the audience was quite hostile to them, and Payne scolded the audience and said (essentially) "You are NOT too cool to boogie!" Johnson put pen to paper (and annihilated that bass line) and the rest is history.

IX/9

PHYLLIS HYMAN

Best known for her statuesque beauty and hits like "You Know How To Love Me" and "Under Your Spell," the Pittsburgh-born Hyman (1949–1995) was nominated for a Tony Award in 1981 for her role in the Duke Ellington–inspired musical *Sophisticated Ladies*.

IX/10

MELBA MOORE

The singer (b. 1945) posed nude in July 1971, photographed by Jack Robinson. The photo, which appeared in the October 15, 1971 issue of *Vogue*, was taken as Moore was touring the country after appearing on Broadway in *Hair* and *Purlie*.

IX/11

TINA TURNER

Almost two years to the day after she left behind one of the most infamous, tumultuous marriages of all time with just 36¢ in her pocket, a reporter from the *Los Angeles Times* was detailing Tina Turner's recent global shopping spree: $27,000 spent in Paris in January; $3,000 in a single afternoon at Neiman-Marcus in Dallas in March; and another $3,000 at Charles Gallay, a boutique in Beverly Hills known for carrying chic, avant-garde styles from Europe before they were made available in the United States. "I'm not an extremist when it comes to clothes," Turner (b. 1939) told the reporter. "When I really get into the mood, I want it all—now—and I just don't like to waste my time. I'll say I want this, this and this and this, and maybe that over there and this, and that's it." She kept her wardrobe under lock and key in two secure walk-in closets in her bedroom, organized according to mood: "sporty, sexy, soft, romantic, transparent, tough, outrageous, and hot." She said of her legendary status in 2005, "I finally accepted that, and it is incredible. I never had as many records as Whitney Houston or Aretha Franklin. But after years and years of work, people finally came to see me in my 60s. I said, 'Why are these people still coming? What is it? I dance and I sing and I make the people feel good. So what?' " She lived up to the freedom she would later describe in her best-selling autobiography, *I, Tina*: "If you are unhappy with anything—your mother, your father, your husband, your wife, your job, your boss, your car—whatever is bringing you down—get rid of it. Because you'll find that when you're free, your true creativity, your true self comes out."

In the lean years after her divorce, Turner paid her rent by cleaning houses before she was able to gain a foothold in the industry again with a series of cabaret shows in Las Vegas in the late 1970s. Her breakthrough solo effort, *Private Dancer*, sold more than ten million copies worldwide and gave the star multiple Grammy Awards and her first solo number one hit, "What's Love Got to Do with It." The song's title inspired the name of the Oscar-nominated film based on her 1986 autobiography, following which she became a truly global star. Although she took a brief foray into movies with unforgettable roles in *Tommy* and *Mad Max: Beyond Thunderdome*, the Nutbush, Tennessee–born international rock icon maintained her primary focus on music and enjoyed sell-out shows worldwide until her self-imposed retirement in 2009. In 2013, she became a Swiss citizen and married her partner of 27 years, Erwin Bach. In an interview a few weeks later with Oprah Winfrey, she spoke of how she planned to earn what she needed to retire and then bow out of the industry without looking back. "I have to be careful how I say this, because the public will get it wrong. When you've waited for something—decades! I went back out after the Ike & Tina days were over—where I was a slave. I had to go back and slave again for myself. And that whole time I [needed to have enough] to take care of my family, and charities, and all of my responsibilities. You have to get yourself in the position so you don't worry about it. I wanted to retire and not worry, and that is what that [final] tour did for me. In the last moments on stage, I had the revelation that, 'This is it, I'm going home now.' In a big way. More than just a house. I was going to a place that I had decided in the last stage of my life that this is where I want to be."

X
RUNWAY REBELS & COVER GIRLS

Naomi Sims (1948–2009) in the photo that appeared on the cover of the October 17, 1969 issue of *Life* magazine.

DIANA VREELAND TOLD HER PROTÉGÉ André Leon Talley in a 1980 *Ebony* interview, "Black models have become the perfect expression and image of elegant fantasy, modern dignity, and the new freedom and confidence all black women have gained in the last ten years." The years she was referring to saw the biggest gains for black models in the industry and these have yet to be matched. Whereas in the 1990s and the dawn of the 21st century you saw one, maybe two, black models on the runway, in the 1970s you saw Billie Blair, Alva Chinn, Mounia, Iman, Peggy Dilliard and other models of color with different complexions and body types.

The most likely place to see black models prior to the 1970s was in Eunice Walker Johnson's *Ebony* Fashion Fair shows, which began in 1958. *Ebony* Fashion Fair was the start for many future stars, including Pat Cleveland, actress Judy Pace, and actor Richard Roundtree. Johnson (1916–2010) was best known as the wife of the late Johnson Publications founder John H. Johnson, but she was a trailblazer in her own right. A graduate of Talladega College, where she majored in sociology and minored in art, she went on to earn a master's degree in social work from Loyola University in Chicago. Johnson's prestigious background was not lost on her future husband, who noted in his 1989 autobiography, *Succeeding Against the Odds: The Autobiography of a Great American Businessman*, "I was not, to put it mildly, one of the great catches of 1940." He continued, "People used to tell Eunice that she was wasting her time keeping company with a young man of doubtful background who was not among the young black professionals who were most likely to succeed. What impressed me about Eunice in comparison with the other young women I had known is that our relationship was not just a romantic fling—it was also a meeting of the minds on what was going on in the world. She was a good listener, sympathetic to my ambitions. She made me feel that maybe I would be somebody one day."

The Johnsons married in 1941 and the next year *Negro Digest*, the first Johnson Publication, was born. *Ebony*, titled by Eunice Johnson, arrived in 1945, and *Jet* came along in 1951. The long-running *Ebony* Fashion Fair began in 1957 as a charitable fashion event with four models doing shows in six cities. The traveling show would help launch the careers of numerous models and go on to raise more than $50 million for various charities around the country.

In 1973, Johnson helped create Fashion Fair Cosmetics after noticing that the *Ebony* Fashion Fair models had to take the time to mix their own makeup for the shows. Fashion Fair ads of the 1970s featured celebrities and a few "regular" women with the tagline, "I'm just. . . ." Leontyne Price, the peerless operatic diva who once said, without a drop of irony, "I totally and completely admit, with no qualms at all, my egomania, my selfishness, coupled with a really magnificent voice," was "just a girl from Laurel, Mississippi," she said in her Fashion Fair ad, adding "I never would have left the church choir."

Yves Saint Laurent was one of the first designers to allow his fashions to be used in the pioneering *Ebony* Fashion Fair shows, but many others had to be convinced. Johnson told the *New York Times* in 2001, "We were the ones who convinced Valentino to use black models in his shows back in the '60s. I was in Paris, and I told him: 'If you can't find any black models, we'll get some for you. And if you can't use them, we're not going to buy from you anymore.' That was before he was famous." Talley, *Vogue*'s editor-at-large, who traveled with Johnson to Paris and Milan to help her select the designs that were featured in *Ebony* Fashion Fair shows, paid tribute to her on NPR's *All Things Considered*. He remembered her as "an extraordinary, loving lady," and said that "Mrs. Johnson wasn't above having a Picasso in her living room but going straight into her kitchen, which was of course state-of-the-art, and making a wonderful pound cake."

The now legendary 1973 fashion show at Versailles brought black models before a wider audience, if only for one spectacular moment in time. It was definitely a watershed moment in the history of black models, and one that has yet to be repeated. Former model and writer Barbara Summers said of that fateful evening, "At Versailles, they had never seen so many flagrantly beautiful black women at one time, so that was a revolution." Summers told NPR in a 2012 interview that the audience that night was used to remoteness from blasé models in European couture. "Black girls changed all that; they plugged fashion into what was happening now, and that meant R&B, rock and roll, dancing, music, and popular culture. They brought the electricity of popular culture into fashion." The designer Paco Rabanne was the first major designer to use black models in his collection in Paris in 1964—and he contended that he paid a steep price for it until black models came into *Vogue* nearly a decade later. He used models like Donyale Luna, whom he presented to Salvador Dali, who then shot her in films. In 1969, several "firsts" in the fashion magazine industry included: Jolie Jones, daughter of music icon Quincy Jones, as the first black model on a *Mademoiselle* cover in March; Jane Hoffman as *Cosmopolitan*'s first black cover model, in June; and Daphne Maxwell (now Daphne Maxwell Reid) as the first black model on the cover of *Glamour*, in October.

After a startling breakthrough in 1967, when she appeared on the cover of the influential fashion supplement of the *New York Times*, Naomi Sims (1948–2009) assumed that signing with one of the top modeling agencies in New York would happen right away. That was not the case. Unable to secure an agent after sending her photos to her art director, she asked Wilhelmina Cooper, the owner of the prestigious Wilhelmina modeling agency, for a favor. "I asked Wilhelmina if I could use her telephone number, and she demurred. But I said, 'What have you got to lose? If anybody calls, you'll get a commission.' I was a saleswoman even at a very early age." Her five-year career combined appearances on the covers of magazines such as *LIFE*, *Cosmopolitan*, and *Essence*, and working with top designers like Halston (who told the *New York Times* in 1974, "Naomi was the first. She was the great ambassador for all black people. She broke down all the social barriers") and Giorgio di Sant'Angelo. Sims started what would become a multi-million dollar wig business in 1973. She also wrote several top-selling beauty books for black women including *All About Health and Beauty for the Black Woman*. Talley wrote after her death in 2007 that without Sims paving the way, "journalists like myself and models would not have been possible."

Beverly Johnson (b. 1952) once said of her historic *Vogue* magazine cover in 1974:

> I didn't know it would be so profound. I just wanted to be on it, because that's where you had to be to be a top model. I didn't realize the significance and change we were embarking on—black women being accepted. Afterwards I knew.

After graduating high school in 1969, Johnson left her hometown of Buffalo, New York to attend Northeastern University in Boston. When she realized that she didn't really want to study law as planned, she decided to try modeling. Her father, who considered modeling "just a soft word for prostitution" was alarmed, but she pressed on and got an interview at *Glamour*, thanks to a friend. "I came to the city with my mother, my little white gloves, and my hair in a topknot, and met with the editors." Even after a coveted 10-page spread in the magazine, Johnson, like Sims before her, was initially unable to find an agency. Soon, however, she was highly sought on the runway and for editorial work, eventually appearing on the cover of over 500 magazines around the world. After her historic appearance on the August 1974 edition of American *Vogue*, the impact of her achievement finally hit her. "I see the inspiration of black women being lifted up all over when they look at me," she told *Newsweek* in 1975, "and that's a super feeling." Johnson was soon to be everywhere: in television commercials and the ubiquitous print ads for Virginia Slims cigarettes with the famous tagline, "You've come a long way, baby." Her wholesome, fresh-faced look was the black version of what the industry called "All-American," and that led her to bread-and-butter spokesperson deals for brands including Avon cosmetics in the late 1970s. In 1981, she wrote her first book, a well-received beauty and health title called *Beverly Johnson's Guide to a Life of Health and Beauty*. Her 1994 book, *True Beauty: Secrets of Radiant Beauty for Women of Every Age and Color*, was even more popular. She also made the perennial model's journey to Los Angeles to try her hand at a career in acting, but soon found that business would be much more rewarding for her. The Beverly Johnson Skin Care System was her first successful beauty line, but her Beverly Johnson Hair Collection, which sells wigs and hairpieces, became even more so. "I was lucky to have been part of something that gave generations of African-American women a sense of belonging that we did not have until then," Johnson said in 2009. "With this privilege came responsibility."

Born Iman Mohamed Abdulmajid in Somalia (in 1955), Iman was a political science major in Nairobi, Kenya who spoke five languages fluently and had never worn makeup or high heels when she was discovered by the American photographer Peter Beard in 1975. On the strength of his recommendation, Iman, the daughter of a Somalian diplomat, was signed, sight unseen, by the Wilhelmina modeling agency. She colluded with Beard in creating what she later called the "Iman mythology." At a press conference, the photographer boasted of "discovering" her in the African jungle, of all places, and they pretended that the multilingual beauty did not speak a word of English. Her flawless beauty, that divine neck, the perfect coppery brown skin, and regal features proved an immediate sensation in the fashion world. In quick succession, she appeared on coveted spreads in American *Vogue* and on the cover of the Italian version of the magazine. Her beauty and intelligence not only made her the muse for major designers like Donna Karan, Calvin Klein, Valentino, and Yves Saint Laurent, but she also began appearing on film and television around the world, including as a wholesome expectant mother on an early episode of *The Cosby Show* and a glamorous damsel-in-distress in the 1980s thriller *No Way Out*.

The designer Michael Kors once aptly described Iman as "an icon for our times," adding that, "It's not just enough to say that she is beautiful or beautifully dressed, although that is a part of the equation. Iman cuts across all ages and experiences. Today women are out there trying to juggle and to make sense of it all. You look at the way Iman looks, her success in business, her need to try new things and to have her own point of view and be a wife and mother—well, not many people have come full circle like that." Iman's full circle now includes an expanding global empire of cosmetics, fashion, and home design. In 2010 Iman was honored by the Council of Fashion Designers (CFDA) with the prestigious Fashion Icon Award, and she works extensively with charitable organizations, especially those that benefit various African nations and children around the world.

X/1

PAT CLEVELAND

Pat Cleveland (b. 1952), photographed in 1977 by Ron Galella. The Harlem-born daughter of painter Lady Bird Cleveland, she began her career as a model in the *Ebony* Fashion Fair shows. André Leon Talley once called her "the Josephine Baker of '70s runway modeling," an apt tribute to her dazzling runway style.

IMAN

Iman (b. 1955), photographed by Patrick Lichfield in 1980. As her star rose in the modeling world, the Somali beauty relished time spent with mentors like the legendary photographer Gordon Parks. "He used to cook for me all the time and then take me to museums," she told *Style*.com in 2011. "He wanted to show me a world outside of fashion."

X/3

DONYALE LUNA

Modeling pioneer Bethann Hardison once said of Luna (1945–1979), "No one looked like her. She was like a really extraordinary species." Born Peggy Ann Freeman in Detroit, she was the first black model to appear on the cover of British *Vogue*, in 1966. She would go on to appear in a few Andy Warhol films including *Screen Test: Donyale Luna* (1964) and *Camp* (1965), as well as Federico Fellini's *Fellini Satyricon* (1970). She also appeared in Otto Preminger's *Skidoo* as the mistress of "God," a crime boss played by none other than comic legend Groucho Marx.

X/4

BEVERLY JOHNSON

Beverly Johnson (b. 1952), photographed by Francesco Scavullo in a ribbed pullover by black designer Scott Barrie in 1974. After becoming the first black woman to appear on the cover of American *Vogue* in 1974, she reflected on the impact of her milestone to *Newsweek* in 1975: "I see the inspiration of black women being lifted up all over when they look at me and that is a great feeling."

X/5

DIANA ROSS

As Diana Ross (b. 1944) touched up her eye shadow in her dressing room in Italy while shooting the movie *Mahogany* in 1975, she made a very keen observation to a visiting reporter from the *Los Angeles Times*. "It's a lot of fun, and while I don't consider the picture really has a moral, I must admit it does have a kind of fairytale ending. But if you think of a real-life Tracy Chambers, she could well be pushing a pram full of babies two years from now. She's going to be unhappy and probably hate the guy. The story is fantasy, but also authentic since any young girl who has grown up in a black neighborhood and has some ambitions wants to get out of the place. She doesn't want to be the woman behind the man, licking envelopes and sticking stamps for the rest of her life. Tracy is vain, tough, sweet, calculating, understanding—more varied, and changing all the time. The part had to be carefully constructed. Both roles nonetheless have some similarity with my own experiences, inasmuch as I'm in show business like Billie and come from the same background as Tracy. Also I've had fame, jewels, big cars, and though I naturally want my career to continue, I'd sometimes like to be down on a farm with my family and lots of grass. I always tell my daughter—the sun will make you grow."

The *Los Angeles Times* profile was illustrated with Ross wearing a body-paint body stocking that she designed for the movie. Although she studied fashion design and costume illustration at Detroit's storied Cass Technical High School, designing the costumes for the film was a controversial move for her. Joan Juliet Buck, a former editor of French *Vogue*, told Constance White, a former editor-in-chief of *Essence*, for White's book *Style Noir*: "Valentino was asked to design the costumes for *Mahogany*, but Diana Ross set off a scandal in Italy (where filming was taking place) when she decided to take charge of her own wardrobe. She ripped everything apart and decided to redesign it herself." Ross had a different take on it, telling *Ebony* magazine in an October 1975 cover story on her that she wanted to design clothes for the film the minute she read the script and realized her character was a budding fashion designer, thinking, "Gee, wouldn't it be something if I could design the clothes." Ross tells the writer that it took some time to convince the film's director and producer, Motown founder Berry Gordy, but once he agreed she went on to design over fifty ensembles with the aid of an assistant. Most of her stage wardrobe was designed by Bob Mackie, who told the *Los Angeles Times* in 1974, "I hear she has a workroom in her house ... She's a frustrated designer herself."

"It's taken me a lifetime to get here," said Ross in her 1993 autobiography *Secrets of a Sparrow*. "I'm not going anywhere."

VI
FOXY MAMAS & DISCO QUEENS

Pam Grier at the height of her fame in 1975.

PAM GRIER (B. 1949), the undisputed queen of blaxploitation films, was optimistic in the now famous *New York* magazine profile on her in 1975 when she spoke of taking film classes at UCLA and setting up her own production company. "I know I can do it. I know I'm big. I read the trades. I can get investors. And I'm going to make movies the way I see fit. No threatless, mindless women. No dumb situations. I know I'm going to have to go slow. But I'm going to sneak up on them little by little and create a monster. This girl isn't just another body for their cameras."

Thirty-two years later, she was telling a different writer for the same magazine, "As a woman of color, you're not going to be the leading lady. Is that going to depress me and make me drink and feel horrible about myself? I can't let that happen to me." She also relayed the lessons she had picked up since her heyday. "The one thing you don't do is that you don't go out there and preach and upset people and make them feel uncomfortable. It's like in martial arts—you don't keep hitting your head on the wall trying to move it." Born in Winston-Salem, North Carolina, Grier was raised on military bases around the world before settling in Denver, Colorado with her family. Initially shy about her looks, Grier was named first runner-up in a beauty pageant and discovered by a Hollywood agent the same night. She immediately moved to Los Angeles and snagged minor roles in low-budget exploitation flicks while working as a switchboard operator and studying at UCLA. The 1973 film *Coffy* made her a star and 1974's *Foxy Brown* turned her into a bona fide icon to feminists and blacks everywhere. Although she was normally shy, her sexy, violent heroines were hardly a stretch for her. "I come from a long line of skillet-throwing women. They were the kind of women who would fight to their last breath before they'd give up their purse to some punk robber." Her career waned a bit in the '80s, but she came roaring back in the '90s after director and devoted fan Quentin Tarantino promised and delivered a role expressly for her, 1997's *Jackie Brown*. More television and film roles followed, along with a best-selling memoir, *Foxy: My Life in Three Acts* (2011).

Prior to portraying the splashy title character in *Cleopatra Jones*, Tamara Dobson (1947–2006), who beat thousands of competitors including top model Naomi Sims for the title role, had a solid career as a model, appearing in *Vogue*, *Harper's Bazaar*, and *Essence* and in ad campaigns for Chanel, Revlon, and Fabergé Tigress. She had bit parts here and there, but the discrepancy between her conviction to take on only dignified roles after *Cleopatra Jones* and her six-foot-one-inch stature combined to stall her acting career, and she never quite gained the same momentum. According to her brother Peter Dobson in an interview following her death, she had a "crushing experience" on one of her final films and decided to leave Hollywood for good. He said that she was very headstrong in her decisions and that she knew, yet didn't know, what an iconic film figure she was. After Dobson replaced Lola Falana as the face of and spokesperson for the Fabergé Tigress fragrance, she told the *Washington Post* in 1978: "I am not good at eyelash fluttering, although I wish I were. But unfortunately, I'm afraid I come from that plain old grit and iron school. Grit your teeth and keep on ironin', honey."

Various interviews with and profiles about Dobson at the height of her career give clues to what this "crushing experience" might have been, because she had definite ideas about what she would and would not do on film. In one 1973 article in *Ebony*, she was very critical of some of the ways that black women were being portrayed in the dawning blaxploitation era—and she named names (or strongly implied them). Considering the attention she was getting after *Cleopatra Jones*, she probably figured that she was on her way to becoming a

Donna Summer (1948–2012) performing in Atlanta, March 1978.

big, big star with her dignity intact. Instead, she left Hollywood and didn't look back. She ignored calls from old friends and offers to get back in the limelight, including a suggestion from her brother that she try her hand at WWE wrestling. At the time of her death at age 59, she resided in New York, where she owned and managed real estate.

The most bankable black female music star of the seventies, Donna Summer (1948–2012), also wrestled with her sex symbol image. "In the beginning it was like being a commodity," Summer told *Rolling Stone* in an interview that was published a few days before a performance in Atlanta in March 1978. "The image and the person got characterized as one and the same, and I was saying, 'No, wait. There's more to me than meets the eye—maybe twenty pounds more.' " Born LaDonna Andre Gaines on New Year's Eve in Boston, she sang with her church choir and then performed with a rock band while a teenager. After graduating high school, she moved to New York to sing and act in theater. Soon after, she found herself in Germany in a production of the Broadway musical *Hair*. Opting to remain in Europe with the show, she performed with the company in Vienna before returning to Germany, where she found work singing background vocals and recording demos. While there, she met and married Helmut Sommer and adopted an Anglicized version of his last name. She was still singing background vocals when she met producer Giorgio Moroder while working on a record by Three Dog Night. She had a European hit with "The Hostage" before scoring in 1975 with the song that would launch her career worldwide, "Love to Love You Baby." Summer was one of the few stars of disco music to survive the era and the subsequent backlash against the genre. She had several hits in the 1980s including her biggest, "She Works Hard for the Money." After being born again as a Christian, she stopped singing her biggest hits until late in life, when she re-embraced her disco days and the music that came with it.

Grace Jones (b. 1948) emerged during the disco era, but was always an entity unto herself. "When people see me, they ask, 'What is it?' " she once said of those who marveled at her metamorphic transformation from Pentecostal preacher's daughter to the gender-bending iconoclast who rose to fame during the androgynous craze of the 1980s. Born in Jamaica, Grace was raised in Syracuse, New York and left home at age 17 to fulfill her appetite to "try everything." She did just about anything she could to belie her upbringing: shaving her head, go-go dancing, becoming a nudist. Eventually she went to Paris, where she modeled for designers like Yves Saint Laurent and Claude Montana. More of a performance artist than a bona fide singer, her nightclub performances in Paris and at New York's fabled Paradise Garage, replete with whips, metal coils, and nearly nude male dancers, are the stuff of legend. She recorded a dozen albums in her career, her biggest hit being the mesmerizing 1981 dance classic "Pull Up to the Bumper." At the height of her fame in the 1980s, she starred in two major films, *Conan the Destroyer* (1984) with Arnold Schwarzenegger and the James Bond film *A View to a Kill* (1985). In 1992 she appeared as the sexy, bizarre model Strangé in Eddie Murphy's *Boomerang*. Grace, who once appeared in a tiger cage gnawing on raw meat, has never felt locked in by her freakish Amazonian image. "I love cartoons," she told *Newsweek* in 1985. "I love the fact that I look like a Walt Disney creation."

XI/1

FREDA PAYNE

Payne (b. 1942 in Detroit) was famed for "Band of Gold" (1970), and her second smash, "Bring the Boys Home" (1971), was banned on Armed Forces Radio at the height of the Vietnam War.

XI/2

SISTER SLEDGE

L–R: Kathy (b. 1959), Debbie (b. 1954), Kim (b. 1957), and Joni (b. 1956), in the U.K. in 1981. The Philadelphia-born sisters were granddaughters of an opera singer and had an actress and singer for a mother and a singer for a father. They had chart-topping hits in the U.K. and Japan before their biggest hit, "We Are Family," in 1979.

XI/3

JAYNE KENNEDY

Photographed in April 1977 during her short-lived NBC TV show, *Cover Girls*. She played Monique Lawrence who was, of course, a secret agent posing as a fashion model. One of the first women to work as a sports announcer, Kennedy (b. 1951) was the first black winner of the Miss Ohio USA contest and a semi-finalist in the 1970 Miss USA pageant.

XI/4

LOLA FALANA

Born in Camden, New Jersey (1942) to a Cuban father and American mother, Lola danced professionally in clubs while in Junior High School. Sammy Davis, Jr. chose her as a featured dancer in *Golden Boy* (1964) on Broadway, and she soon earned a recording contract. In the late '60s she became famous as the Black Venus in Italy, where she'd made three spaghetti Westerns (speaking Italian). In America Lola appeared in the first series of the *New Bill Cosby Show* (1972–73) and a string of other prime time shows. In the late 1970s she was the Queen of Las Vegas and the highest-paid woman in the city. Since the late 1980s she has battled against multiple sclerocis.

AFTERWORD

LOOKING BACK

I KNEW THAT I WANTED to open this book with a portion of Pearl Cleage's *We Speak Your Names* because that refrain, "we speak your names," would go through my mind with every photograph, story, or anecdote I found that told the story of the women who fill the book's pages. With every rare story or photograph about Lena Horne or Dorothy Dandridge, and with every gem about Ethel Waters or Rose Morgan that had not been shared for decades, if at all, I thought "we speak your names." I wanted to immortalize them, to have a permanent record of these women who inspired legends and, in many cases, became legends themselves. My hope is that the glamour and achievements celebrated in *Vintage Black Glamour* serve as a constant reminder of these magical women who were born of magical women, who truly built the bridge across which so many of us can now walk with ease and comfort. Their style, grace, and elegance were magnified by their struggles and triumphs; by the impact they had in their professional fields and on culture throughout the world. Incredibly, many of the same battles they fought for visibility and equality are still being waged today but, at the same time, many barriers that probably seemed light years away from being dismantled, if that were possible at all, have long since been kicked over.

Even with barriers gone, though, it is not uncommon for people to tell me that they have never seen a certain picture or heard a particular piece of information about the subjects covered in *Vintage Black Glamour*, even when that person is very well known. While, due to the nature of a book like this there are only so many great photographs that can be included, it was really important to me to include some of the lesser known and unknown women here. So some familiar faces, while named, may not be pictured due to lack of space not interest. My hope is that by telling the stories of these women (and eventually the men, too), people will see the hard work and sacrifice that went into the foundations that they laid. I hope that when modern-day performers sing songs or wear outfits that were inspired by the innovations of these legends, respectful recognition is given. I hope that there is enjoyment and sheer pleasure to be had from gazing upon the undeniable evidence of the brilliance and splendor of these women who, while pursuing their own creative and professional goals, inspired and enlightened generations to come.

My lovely aunt Mildred Taylor (left) and her lifelong friend Queenesther James in their modeling days in Newark, New Jersey in the early 1950s. This photo is from James's personal collection and was taken by Wells Raney, a photographer for the *Afro-American* newspaper.

ROLL OF HONOR

The publishers gratefully acknowledge the contribution of everyone listed below, whose generous support has helped bring this project to fruition.

Pam "The Texas Tea Queen" Aaron | Saleemah Abdul-Ghafur | Andrea Natalie Abrams | Kari Adams | Rita & Joe Adefope | Afrobella | Oghenekome Aganga-Williams | Ediyie Akpan | Denise Alden | Janice Alder | Essie Grace Alexander | Maia Marlessa Alexander | Ayn Allen | Candace Allen | Mama Alto | Annemarie Adzokor Anang | Adrienne M. Anderson | Corinne Anderson | Crystal Anderson | Estelle Anderson | Marguerite Daniels Anderson | Martin Anderson | Michael G. Anderson | Patricia Andrews-Keenan | Camisha Antoinette | Salima Appiah-Duffell | Yolanda R. Arrington | Gwenda Asher | Julian Asion | Lindsey Atkinson | Nathania Atkinson | Bertram Attles | Aretha C. Augustine | Shameeka Shy Ayers | Danielle LeAnn Ayers | Basannya Babumba | Annushka P. Baker | Toshiana Baker | Gwynn Montil Baldwin | Jessica Banks | Dr. Cheryle Baptiste | Jenay Jackson Barbee | Linda Holloman Barnes | Robert R. Barney, Sr. | Renee M. Baron | Belinda Bates | LaTashi Battle | Sean & Brenda Battle | Nichole Bazemore | Nyla Olivia Beard | Lisa Bell | Marsha Bennett-Gainer, M.A. | Jamyla & Pierre Bennu | Daisy Bermudez | Marisol Beswick | Pamela Bethel | Kendra Beverley | Mia Birdsong | Denise L. Blackwell | Nicole Blades | Ronald A. Blake | Tracy Blakely | Yaba Blay | Rose L. Bligen | Natika S. Blount | Tamara Y. Boggs | Boise Public Library | Paula Peebles Bonds | Doreen Bonner-Midder | Paula E. Boothe | Michon Boston | Lamouria Boyd | Deborah Bozeman | Tracey Branch | Andrea L.J. Breath | Melanie Hall Briggs | Monique Brizz-Walker | Misha Samone Brooker | Sharon Scott Brooking | Charles E. & Ruth C. Brown | Kathleen Brown | Kedma Brown | Kim Sanders Brown | Milton Brown | Shaunte Brown | Tanya Nicole Ballard Brown | Tara Rose Brown | Tavari Taylor Brown | Apryl Bruce | Sue Bruno | Jordan Bryant | Louis & Maya Bullock | A'Lelia Bundles | Adrienne Burch | Dondrie Burnham | Journey & Denisha Burns | Olutosin & Farran Burrell | Angie Burrus | Corneilia Burston-Orr | Dr. & Mrs. James Butler, III | James E. Butler, Esq. | Nicole Byars | Joyce Hilton Bransford Byrd | Kevin Byrne | Nathalie A. Cadet-James | Miezi Dolores Savina Cafasso | Tiffany Cain | Starla Caldwell | Candice Nicole Canteen | Catrice A. Canty-Pope | Chekena "Kena" Carter | Courtney C. Carter, M.D. | Marcus Carter & Leslie Jackson | Michael W. Casey | Bernadette Marion Chapman | Brithani Chardae | Dominique Christina Charles | Nyieta Charlot & Anjolie Charlot | Dr. D.J. Childs, D.S.T. | Jamia S. Chislom | Stephanie A. Clanton | Angela D. Clark | Carlo Jerome Clarke | David Clarke | Ann Ruth Davis Claybrooks | Christa Lynne Clemons | Chelsea Coates | Lisa Coffman | Ebonē S. Colbert-Taylor | Titania Altius Cole | Adia Burriss Coleman | Charlotte L. Coleman | Jennifer Coleman | LaToya G. Coley | Constance S. Collier-Mercado | Tiffany N. Collins | Cassye D. Cook | Kato Cooks | Simone Cooks | Chandra Y. Cooper | Charrell Cooper | Misty Copeland | Brenda Lee Cornelius | Jacqueline Couti | Cynthia Cowdery | Kareen Craig | Njeri Craig | Nandi A.Grazette Crawford | Carl J. Cruz | Thomas Lee Cunningham IV | Dr. Karen Curls | Nadine Joy Curry | Marlon Vernon Davids | Dwayne C. Davis | Geraldine "Ms Lucy" Davis | India Davis | Lisa E. Davis | Nicole Titilayo Davis | Aliah Davis-McHenry | Russella L. Davis-Rogers | Adrienne Dawes | William I. Dawson | Cheryl F. Deane | Leo Joseph DeCoud, Sr. | Linda DeHart | Leola "Roscoe" Dellums | Alycsa DeMarinis | Monica C. Dennis | Natashia Deon | Coco Deville | Zaria Diallo | Amina Dickerson | Barbara A. Dickerson | Iris Dillon | Brianna Dixon | Carol Ann Dixon | Hilary Grant Dixon | Jessie Mae Jones Doherty | Chakowa Donaldson | Monique S. Dopwell | Genesha K. Dorris | Lauren L. Dorsey | Andrea Downing | Danielle M. DuCré | De Angela L. Duff | Mr. Ronald Alvin Dunlap | Ms. Veronica Nechele Dunlap | Andy Dunn | Sir Tim Easton | Carolyn Edgett | Dr. Ashanti Edwards | Penelope S. Edwards-Carter | Adasha M. Elam | Debra Beth Eldridge | Tasheaya & Scott Ellison | Melanie Lynn Ennis | Esse Purse Museum & Store | Sefora Estifanos-Haddish | Christine Madden Evans | Maisha Everhart | Anthony Exum | Kristin Fance | Yvette Armanda Fibleuil | Camille Wright Felton | Jay Allan Fenton | Ashley Ferrell | Brenda Stith Finch | Margaret Finch | Bernette E. Fisher | Melanie Forbis | Christina Michelle Ford | Curtis Ford | Dr. James E. Ford, III & Mrs. Kwanda Ford | Yvette Monique Ford | Monita Ford-Shaw | Kerri Forrest | Richardene Forrest-Thweatt | Cat Forsyth | LaTanya Marie Fountain | Michael Christopher Fountain | Vanessa N. Francis | Candace Franklin | Sheena D. Franklin | Autumn D. Frazier | Pearline Francine Friis | Tracey Friley | Alphonso Fudge | Deborah A. Futrell | Roxie Lydia Gamble | Toni Garcia | Martha Garvey, Jr. | Ann-Marie Gayle | Sanford E. Gaylord | Thomas Gibian | Courtney Gilbert | Miss. India Jane Gill | Tiffany M. Gill, Ph.D | Lesley Gillard | Scott Gisler | Mayme Eloyce Gist | Kim Golden-Malmgren | Jérôme Gourvennec | Eboni J. Govan | Clarrette Gray | Felice N. Gray-Kemp | Jonathan Green | Tandy Green | William M. Green | Aliah Greene | LeVan Greene | Shana Griffin | Valerie Gloria Jean "Glow" Griffin | Laura P. Grissom | Kali Diana Grosvenor | Tamika Nicole Guess | Sonya F. Hadley | Louise Haigler | Joyce L. Hall | Chris Anthony Hamilton | Doreene Hamilton | Minnie Hamilton | Jade C. Hampton | Janet Simpson Hardaway | Nadia Joyce & Ava "J" Hardy | Janice Clemons Harley | Charla Harlow | Debra L. Harris | Barbara Harris | Sheila E. Harris | Willie Harris, Jr. | Davon D.E. Hatchett-Robinson | Stephanie Haughton-Campbell | Annie Hawkins | Kimberly Hawthorne | Cheryl L. Hay | Tamara Hayes | Adrienne Heim | Ray Hemachandra | Darnica Monike Hernandez | La-Shawn Hill | Gaberial Hill-Braun | Lisa Hill-Corley | Deborah J. Hines | Courtney C. Hobson | S.M. Holcey | Briallen Hopper | Andrea Horne | Margaret Horton | Sara Horton | Kellee & Horace Hough | Amelia Hoy | Gary A. Huddleston | Vanessa Hulme | Sharon Sillet Hutlas | Debra Hutto | Adrena C. Ifill | Uchenna Ikonne | Neal Izumi | Simone Jack | Ravi Pascal Jacks | Daniella Jackson | Donna Monifa Jackson | Sandra Jackson | Sharon Purdie Jackson | Mrs. Sirelda Jackson | Stephanie Jackson, M.D. | Tramia Jackson | Martin & Akieva Jacobs | Miss Shayna R. Jeffers | Senora Janae Jelks | Mrs. Camille Conner Jenkins | Isabella Sophie Castano Jessup | Alonzo Johnson | Art Johnson | In Memoriam, Claudia B. Johnson | Derreck & Renee Johnson | H. & A. Johnson | Kenasha Johnson | Kimberley Ann Johnson | Kimberly Sue Johnson | Michelle Shere Johnson | Yewande Johnson | Tonya L. Jones | Anthony David Jordan | Sharon James Jordan | Ryalon Katril & Zara Noel | Abigail Rosanne Kelly | Erica Kennedy | Takeisha Kennemore | Thaysha A. King | Renee King-Straker | Lauretha "Laurie" Knight | Joelle LaGuerre | Taneshia Nash Laird | Harold D. Lamar, Jr. | Dawn Landon | Justine Larbalestier | Sheniqua "Nini" Larkin | Utausha Elie Laster |

Saida Mustakeem Latigue | Nina Lattimore | Brittnee Lavender | Carol Lavern | Jason Lavinder | Katharine Isobel Lawden | Molly Lee | Naomi S. Leotta | Denitria Nyree Lewis | Shannon Lewis | Alysha Light | Tammy K. Ligon | Diandra Nicole Linder | Angela Linton-Miller | Adrian Michelle Lipscombe | Regina Lites | Sharon D. Lloyd | Adrienne Lockhart | Amelia Loren Smith | Kim Love | Latriece Love | George C. Mable | Joanne Madhere | Anita Smith Madison | Sonia A. Madison | Roy & Val Magett | Eudald Magri | Tracy Malcolm | Truly Mae Marks | Bennie L. Martin | Cheryl L. Martin | Toribio E. Martin, Jr. | Zena Martin | Allyson R. Martinez | Bianca Mason | Floydetta McAfee | Yolanda McClamb | Cynthia Y. McCoy | Yolanda McCutchen | Elzina McDaniel | Michael Mcdonel | Eumikia G. McElroy | Greta Chapin Mcgill | Warren "Tony" McGriff, Sr. | Delfon & Leisa McSpadden | Jennifer Rose McZier | Suzanne Melton | Madalena Pedro Miala | Marie Michael | Debra D. Miller | Evelyn Henry Miller | Nicolle E. Miller | Hazel Milton & Martha Penrice | Judith Alicia Mims | Ariyan Mitchell | Catherine E. Mitchell | Jazmyn Mitchell | Laurie Mitchell | Toya Mitchell | Vivien Mitchell | Robyn Monroe | Patrice A. Monteiro | Elsa Perez Moore | Sharon Moorehead | Michael Moorman | Hilda M. Morgan | Kelsey & Jordan Morgan | Kendall Morgan | Charlotte Morgan-Nwokenna | Lisa Hollinger Morin | Evelyn J. Moses | Thembisa S. Mshaka | Domba Muamba | Keenya Murray | Tracy Murrell | Mildred L. Nance | Consuela Nance-Rankin | Milton H. Nash | Miakka Natisse | Andrew & Vanessa Neal | Lygia Nealmailo | Gayle Nelson | Rock & Dede Newman | Dr. Valerie Rene'e Newsome | Dr. Darrell M. Newton | Tiffany Nicholson-Horton | Nichelle Nickles | Ngeri Nnachi-Azuewah | Kimberly Noel | Kendra Perkins Norwood | Liesl K. Nottingham | Danielle McCray Ntim | Crystal Obiukwu | Zenaida Tawa Odom | Arlene McCormick Ogletree | Donna E. Oldham | Marci Bailey Overstreet | Terry Lynn & Sarah Marguerite Overton | Oyinlola Oyelayo | Yolanda Perry Paige | Anika Myers Palm | Mrs. Brandi Shamara Parker | Temitope Omosegbon Parrish | Gail Parson-Cooper | Karyn Parsons | Nile Pasha | Nicholas Patrick | Samata Pattinson | David S. Pearson, Jr. | Aimee Danielle Peoples | Sharon A. Peppers | Mrs. Mary E. Perry | Jessica Peterson | Shaka Ané Phillips | Victor & Crystal Pierre | Brenda M. Plummer | Mrs. Raphael H. Plunkett | Michael D. Poe | Antoinette L. Poindexter | Yardly Pollas | Allison Nicole Poole | Siobhan Porter | Retha Powers | Doris Pradieu | Michelle Earlington Pramuka | Clyde Prescod | June A. Price | Joi Maria Probus | Dana J. Prophet | Kristen Slater Prophet | Trevor & Sonya Pryce | Nina Pupikofer | Jasmine Q. | Lisa S. Quinn | Madeline Murphy Rabb | Marini Ramee | Courtney Michelle Ramsey | Johari M. Rashad, Ph.D. & Chekesha W. Rashad, M.S., C.M.P. | Raven | Rebecca Raven | Amirah Raveneau-Bey | Shirae D. Ravenell | Taiasha Ravenell | Rachelle Angeline Ray | Candice Raynor | Lhatoya Reed | Shauna Reeder & Andres Gonzalez | James Rayvon Reeves | Kai M. Reevey | Kyndra "Binkie" Reevey | Nakena R. Reich | Deanna Reid | Marian Myers Rembert | Sonya Reynolds | Radiah Rhodes | Alexandra & Jacqueline Rice in Honor of Pamela Rice | Nichola Richards | Roxann R. Richards | Peter Jason Riley | Meghan N. Rivers | Kalia Roach | Kendra N. Roberts | Traci R. Roberts | Arlene Quinn Robillard | Dr. Irving W. Robinson, Sr. | Leslie G. Robinson | Loretta Robinson | Traci Michelle Robinson | Nicole Robinson-Hamilton | Elaine Rock | Mrs. Juanita Ross | Susan J. Ross | Pasquale Virginie Rotter | Da'Shawn Roundtree | Nadine Persaud Rowbotham | A. Rowe | Amanda Royes | Leah A. Rudolfo | Joshua Safran | Jenn Sagaria | Becky Sales | Carmen Sanders | Bernadette Sargeant | Deborah J. Saunders | Sherryl Saunders | Byron Scott | Dr. Charneta Claudetta Scott | Shandra Aimee Scott | Komali Scott-Jones | Anika Crystal Seals | Erica K. Senat | Gia Holmes Sharp | Brandi R. Sharpe | Shorefront Legacy Center | Faye Lorente Shyllon | Sarah Lee Siebolt | Eve Siegel | Aisha "Lyfe" Silva | Christine N. Simmons | Jessica A. Simmons | Vanessa Broussard Simmons | Janelle Singleton | Piper Slaymaker | James P. Sloan | Annette-Marie Smith | Ayesha Nichelle Smith | Brandon Van Smith | Carl Smith | Rev. & Mrs. Clarence Smith | Lisa Smith | Rachel Lynley Smith | Amy L. Sommers | Sonofellis | Tiffanni Spann | Kimberlee Spears | Alexis Manya Spraic | LaRita Sprott | Hon. Cheryl A. Starks (Ret.) | Sharon M. Starnes | Juneko Steele | Crystal Gail Stocks | Ms. Marie Olive Stoddart | Deborah E. Stoicheff | Allison Strickland | Michelle D. Strickland, Esq. | Barbara Summers | Queion Swift | Janice Lynn Sykes | Carla J. Tabb | Mariahadessa Ekere Tallie | Robin Bryson Talmadge | Victoria Tapscott | Dawn Tarter-Brewton | Denton Taylor | Kyle Everett Taylor | Sonya Robinson Taylor | Cecile L. Thalley | Nathalie Thandiwe | Jillian Theresa | Bonnie Thomas | Kenyatta Thomas | Star S. Thomas | Tabetha Thomas | Kurt Thometz | Julee D. Thompson | Kisha M. Thompson | Pamela J. Thompson | Vanessa Thompson | Angela Thrasher | Tulani Milan Titley | Anna Mary Adams Titus | Jessica Toland | Joelette Tylan Toler | Monya Tomlinson | Jacqueline E. Trescott | Tanya Angelina Trowell | Paula J. Truss | Aleim Celeste Tucker | Rakia Turner | Patricia L. Turner, M.D., F.A.C.S. | Dane Twining | Ewunike A. Vallier | Zakiya S. Vallier | Cheryl VanHook | Tiffany Vazquez | LaWanda Velez | Gary D. Veney | Vicki Mabrey | April W. | Tricia Elam Walker | Morgan Wall-Stewart | Gretchen Ward Waller | Jorge Walsh | Nicole Cowan Walters | Angela D. Walton | Roxanne Janae Walton | Janae D. Walton-Green | Jennifer Marie Ward | Dr. Adella D. Gaston Washington | Marjorie C. Washington | Nyle Washington | Sharon Washington | Dr. Billye Sankofa Waters | Chantel R. Watkins | M. Theresa Watkins | Victoria R. Watkins, Esq. | Dr. Kristina Yvette Watkins-Mormino | Tomecia Nichole Weaver | Dr. Scena B. Webb | Tia J. Webb | Barbara Webb-Edwards & Alvin Edwards | Cassaundra Webster | Gail Berry West | Amber Wheeler | Ruby Lee Wheeler | David M. Whettstone | Raphael White | Cassandra Renee Wiggins | Connie Lynn Williams | Denise Kimberly Williams | Gail Dixon Williams | Mikhaela' Williams | Nicole Amanda Williams | Rachel Aminah Williams | Tasha Williams | Tina Williams | Tracyann Williams | Pamela Williams-Lacy | Catrina Williams-Smith | Alicia Verna Wilson | Charlene Sophia Wilson | Janean Wilson | Tammy Camille Wilson | Lillian Wimbish | Windslider | Hilary L. Winfield | Sherrilyn Winkfield | Janey Winterbauer | Rodney F. Witcher | Daisy Withers | Gertrude D. & James H. Wooten, Jr. | Abigail Wray | Jennifer LaJuan Wright | Michael "The Mentor" Wright | Carol Wyatt | Melville Q. Wyche, Jr., M.D. | Nicole Wycislo | Catherine Mims Yamaguchi | Chenita Dix Young | Ken Young | Sherice Yvette | Zaira Nadygail Zafra

BIBLIOGRAPHY

Opening Quote

Pearl Cleage, *We Speak Your Names: A Celebration*. New York: One World/Ballantine, 2006.

Introduction

Irving Townsend, "Ellington in Private", *Atlantic Monthly*, May 1975.

Diahann Carroll, *The Legs Are the Last to Go*. New York: Amistad, 2008.

Margaret Tynes phone interview by Nichelle Gainer, May 2003.

Chapter I – Tall, Tan, & Terrific

Paula Giddings, *When And Where I Enter: The Impact of Black Women on Race and Sex in America*. New York: HarperCollins, 1984.

Brenda Dixon-Gottschild, *Waltzing in the Dark: African American Vaudeville and Race Politics in the Swing Era*. New York: Palgrave Macmillan, 1999.

Donald Bogle, *Bright Boulevards, Bold Dreams: The Story of Black Hollywood*. New York: One World Books, 2005.

Daphne A. Brooks, *Bodies in Dissent: Spectacular Performances of Race and Freedom, 1850–1910*. Durham, N.C.: Duke University Press, 2006.

Deborah Gray White, *Too Heavy a Load: Black Women in Defense of Themselves, 1894–1994*. New York: W.W. Norton & Company, 1999.

Noliwe Rooks, *African American Women's Magazines and the Culture that Made Them*. New Brunswick: Rutgers University Press, 2004.

Nadine George Graves, *The Royalty of Negro Vaudeville: The Whitman Sisters and the Negotiation of Race, Gender and Class in African American Theater 1900–1940*. New York: Palgrave Macmillan, 2000.

Bill Reed, *Hot from Harlem: Twelve African American Entertainers, 1890–1960*. Jefferson, N.C.: McFarland & Co., 2009.

Charlene B. Regester, *African-American Actresses: The Struggle for Visibility 1900–1960*. Bloomington: Indiana University Press, 2010.

Nella Larsen, *Quicksand and Passing*, ed. Deborah E. McDowell. New Brunswick: Rutgers University Press, 1986.

David Krasner, "Black Salome: Exoticism, Dance, and Racial Myths", in *African American Performance and Theater History: A Critical Reader*, ed. Harry J. Elam, Jr. and David Krasner. Oxford: OUP, 2001.

Harlem Renaissance Lives: From the African American National Biography, ed. Henry Louis Gates, Jr., Evelyn Brooks Higginbotham. Oxford: OUP, 2009.

Constance Valis Hill and Margaret Morrison, "Alice Whitman and the Whitman Sisters' Legacy". *http://atdf.org/bios/WhitmanSistersBio.html*

Paul Galloway, "Etta Moten Gave Film a New Image: Today She Stars on the Civic Stage", *Chicago Tribune*, February 7, 1989.

Oscar Michaeux, "The Negro and the Photoplay", *Half Century*, May 1919.

"Etta Moten Barnett, 102; 'Porgy and Bess' Star Sang at the White House", obituary, *Los Angeles Times*, January 5, 2004.

Barbara Summers, *Black and Beautiful: How Women of Color Changed The Fashion Industry*. New York: Amistad, 1998.

SPECIAL FEATURE: JOSEPHINE BAKER

Josephine Baker and Jo Bouillon, *Josephine*, trans. Mariana Fitzpatrick. New York: Harper and Row, 1977. (Originally published as *Josephine*. Paris: Robert Lafont-Opera Mundi, 1976.)

Bennetta Jules-Rosette, *Josephine Baker in Art and Life: The Icon and the Image*. Champaign: University of Illinois Press, 2007.

Chapter II – Sepia Dreamgirls, Pin-Ups, & Hollywood Starlets

David Park, "CAESAR, LOIS TOWLES", Handbook of Texas Online (http://www.tshaonline.org/handbook/online/articles/fcaeu). Published by the Texas State Historical Association.

Bogle 2005.

Stephanie Capparell, *The Real Pepsi Challenge: The Inspirational Story of Breaking the Color Barr*. New York: Free Press, 2007.

SPECIAL FEATURE: LENA HORNE

Gail Lumet Buckley, *The Hornes: An American Family*. New York: Knopf, 1986.

James Gavin, *Stormy Weather: The Life of Lena Horne*. New York: Atria, 2010.

SPECIAL FEATURE: DOROTHY DANDRIDGE

Ebony, June 1962, March 1986

Oakland Tribune, 1962

Horace Newcomb, editor, *Encyclopedia of Television*, Fitzroy Dearborn, 2004t

Bill Reed, *Hot from Harlem: Twelve African American Entertainers, 1890–1960*, McFarland & Co, 2009

Bogle, 2005

Donald Bogle, *Dorothy Dandridge: A Biography*, Amistad 1999.

Chapter III – Wives & Socialites

Nancy Beck Young, *Lou Hoover: Activist First Lady*. Lawrence: University Press of Kansas, 2004.

Shelley Stokes-Hammond, *Pathbreakers: Oscar Stanton DePriest and Jessie L. Williams DePriest*. The White House Historical Association. http://www.whitehousehistory.org/whha_shows/depriest-tea-incident/african-american-congress.html

"Edna Mae Robinson, 86, Dancer and Boxer's Wife", obituary, *New York Times*, May 7, 2002.

"Remembering Sugar Ray: Edna Mae Robinson recalls the glitter and the pain of her past", *Ebony*, December 1989.

Al Sullivan, "Living with a living legend: Ray Robinson Jr. remembers his famous boxing father", *Hudson Reporter*, August 1, 2012.

"Oprah Talks To Camille Cosby", *O, The Oprah Magazine*, May 2000.

Bogle 2005.

Dixon-Gottschild 1999.

Barbara Summers 1998.

"Nat 'King' Cole's Widow Maria Cole Visits Charlotte Hawkins Brown Museum", North Carolina Department of Cultural Resources, 2008. http://news.ncdcr.gov/2008/06/11/nat-king-coles-widow-maria-cole-visits-charlotte-hawkins-brown-museum/

Jessie Carney Smith, ed., *Notable Black American Women: Book II*, (Maria Cole). Detroit: Thomson Gale, 1996.

Chapter IV – Beauty & Fashion Entrepreneurs

Michael Henry Adams, "Some Harlem Women Who Helped Make Black Beautiful", March 2013. http://mrmhadams.typepad.com/blog/2013/03/some-harlem-women-who-helped-make-black-beautiful.html

A'Lelia Bundles, *On Her Own Ground: The Life and Times of Madam C.J. Walker*. New York: Scribner, 2001.

Philip Scranton, *Beauty and Business: Commerce, Gender and Culture in Modern America*. New York: Routledge, 2000.

"House of Beauty: Rose-Meta Salon Is Biggest Negro Beauty Parlor in the World", *Ebony*, May 1946.

A'Lelia Bundles, "My Grandmother's Harlem Renaissance Wedding", *Harlem World*, December 2, 2011.

Rosemary E. Reed Miller, *Threads of Time, The Fabric of History: Profiles of African American Dressmakers and Designers, 1850 to the Present*. Washington, D.C.: Toast & Strawberries Press, 2007.

"Geri Major, Dean of American Designers: Frail New Yorker has spent 50 years creating fashions for top society", *Ebony*, December 1966.

Chapter V – Prima Donna Assolutas

Joyce Aschenbrenner, *Katherine Dunham: Dancing a Life*. Champaign: University of Illinois Press, 2002.

Rosalyn M. Story, *And So I Sing: African American Divas of Opera and Concert*. New York: Harper Paperbacks, 2000.

Brian Lanker, *I Dream a World: Portraits of Black Women Who Changed America*. New York: Stewart, Tobri & Chang, 1989.

Yaël Tamar Lewin, *Night's Dancer: The Life of Janet Collins*. Middletown, CT: Wesleyan University Press, 2011.

Alex Ross, "Othello's Daughter", *New Yorker*, July 29, 2013.

Chapter VI – Scandalous Glamour

Langston Hughes, *The Big Sea*. New York: Knopf, 1940, p.177–8, 180–81.

Bricktop with James Haskins, *Bricktop*. New York: Atheneum, 1983, p.116.

Carl Van Vechten, "Portraits of the Artists", *Esquire*, 58:6 (1962), p.257

Van Vechten to Langston Hughes, 29 Nov. 1939, in Emily Bernard, ed., *Remember Me to Harlem: The Letters of Langston Hughes and Carl Van Vechten 1925–1964*,. New York: Knopf, 2001, pp.156–7

Emmett George Price, ed., *Encyclopedia of African American Music, Volume 3*. Santa Barbara: Greenwood, 2010.

Holt to Van Vechten, 20 Sept. 1927, Van Vechten Papers, Beinecke Library, Yale University.

Bogle 2005.

SPECIAL FEATURE: EARTHA KITT

Benedict College students find Ms. Kitt's birth certificate, in Rob Hoerburger, "Eartha Kitt, A Seducer of Audiences, Dies at 81", obituary, *New York Times*, December 25, 2008.

Financial participation and letters to southern theater owners regarding "Anna Lucasta" in 1958, in Alan Gevinson, *Within Our Gates: Ethnicity in American Feature Films, 1911–1960*. Berkley: University of California Press, 1997.

"Ms. Kitt spoke four languages and sang in seven." in Rob Hoerburger, "Eartha Kitt, A Seducer of Audiences, Dies at 81", obituary, *New York Times*, December 25, 2008.

Ms. Kitt told Ebony in 1993, "I trust the dirt…", in Richette Hayward, "Older and Better: Earth Kitt at Sixtysomething", *Ebony*, October 1993.

Eartha Kitt telephone interview with Nichelle Gainer, 2001.

Eartha Kitt's bird nest in Anita Sethi, "Pieces of Me", *Guardian*, November 27, 2008.

Chapter VII – Jazz Singers, Musicians, & Writers

Farah Jasmine Griffin, *If You Can't Be Free, Be A Mystery: In Search of Billie Holiday*. New York: Random House, 2002.

Sarah Vaughan biography accessed on *Jazz: A Film* by Ken Burns on PBS.org, from Barry Kernfeld, ed., *The New Grove Dictionary of Jazz*. Oxford: OUP, 2003. http://www.pbs.org/jazz/biography/artist_id_vaughan_sarah.htm

Ella Fitzgerald biography accessed on *Jazz: A Film* by Ken Burns on PBS.org, from Kernfeld 2003.http://www.pbs.org/jazz/biography/artist_id_fitzgerald_ella.htm

SPECIAL FEATURE: BLANCHE CALLOWAY

Alyn Shipton, *Hi-De-Ho: The Life of Cab Calloway*. Oxford: OUP, 2010.

Gilbert Gaster, "Clyde Bernhardt", *Storyville*, no.44, December 1972, 58.

Chapter VIII – Movie Stars, Theater, & TV Pioneers

Diahann Carroll quote from Carroll 2008.

Interview with Judy Pace by Roger Ebert, January 10, 1969. http://www.rogerebert.com/interviews/interview-with-judy-pace

Interview with Abbey Lincoln by Roger Ebert, August 18, 1968. http://www.rogerebert.com/interviews/abbey-lincoln-you-cant-really-tell-the-story-until-everyone-gets-on-the-stage

Diana Sands interview, *Look* magazine, January 9, 1968.

Diana Sands interview, *New York Times*, December 31, 1967.

Susan Fales-Hill, *Always Wear Joy: My Mother Bold and Beautiful*. New York: Harper Collins, 2003, p.169.

Bogle 2005.

Matt Mazur, "Giving Us Something We Can Feel: An Interview with Lonette McKee", *Pop Matters*, August 12, 2010. http://www.popmatters.com/pm/feature/129327-giving-us-something-we-can-feel-an-interview-with-lonette-mckee/

SPECIAL FEATURE: DIAHANN CARROLL

Louie Robinson, "Have Blacks Really Made It in Hollywood?", *Ebony*, June 1975.

Charles L. Sanders, "Diahann Carroll: How death of her youthful husband changed her life,", *Ebony*, November 1979.

Carroll 2008.

Chapter IX – Soul Sisters, Perfect Angels, & Rock And Roll Divas

Mary Wilson quoted in Ruth La Ferla, "Dare to Be Supreme", *New York Times*, December 17, 2006.

Maxine Powell on The History Makers. http://www.thehistorymakers.com/biography/maxine-powell-40

WGBH Interview with Maxine Powell, Part 1: http://openvault.wgbh.org/catalog/e72b1c-interview-with-maxine-powell-part-1-of-2/print

WGBH Interview with Maxine Powell, Part 2: http://openvault.wgbh.org/catalog/bf1194-interview-with-maxine-powell-part-2-of-2/print

Richard Goldstein, "Coiffed and spangled Aretha Franklin", *Vogue*, August 15, 1968.

"Gowns by Black designers, including Stephen Burrows", *Ebony*, October 1974.

Nikki Giovanni, *The Collected Poetry of Nikki Giovanni 1968–1998*. New York: William Morrow, 2003.

SPECIAL FEATURE: TINA TURNER

Jennifer Seder, "Tina Turner", *Los Angeles Times*, June 2, 1978.

"Ike and Tina Turner", *Ebony*, May 1971.

"Oprah Talks To Tina Turner", *O, The Oprah Magazine*, May 2005.

Chapter X – Runway Rebels & Cover Girls

Sylvia A. Harvey, "Beverly Johnson: 35 Years After Her Historic Vogue Cover", *The Daily Voice*, August 11, 2009. http://thedailyvoice.com/voice/2009/08/post-8-002175.php

Ted Morgan, "I'm the Biggest Model, Period", *New York Times*, magazine, August 17, 1975.

Charla Krupp, "Four Supermodels Tell It Like It Was", *Glamour*, April 1989.

Teri Agins, "Iman: Not Just Another Pretty Face", *New York Times*, June 4, 2010.

Iman, *I Am Iman*. New York: Universe Publishing, 2001.

SPECIAL FEATURE: DIANA ROSS

Camille Duhe, "People Are Talking About: Diana Ross", *Vogue*, March 1, 1978.

Summers 1998.

Constance C.R. White, *StyleNoir: The First How-To Guide to Fashion Written With Black Women in Mind*. New York: Perigee/Penguin Books, 1998.

Chapter XI – Foxy Mamas & Disco Queens

Mark Jacobson, "Pam Grier: Sex Goddess of The Seventies?", *New York*, May 19, 1975.

Mikal Gilmore, "Donna Summer: Is There Life After Disco?", *Rolling Stone*, March 23, 1978.

Dennis Nishi, "Star Trek's Nichelle Nichols on How Martin Luther King Jr. Changed Her Life", *The Wall Street Journal* Speakeasy blog, January 17, 2011.

Nichelle Gainer, "*Honey* Icon: Lola Falana", *Honey* magazine, December 2001, p.114.

INDEX OF IMAGES & CREDITS

Listed in the form of subject, image credit, and page number.

ACKNOWLEDGEMENTS

To my grandmother Louise Murphy, who has always cared the most.

I WOULD LIKE TO THANK MY AUNTS, Mildred Taylor and Margaret Tynes whose lives piqued my curiosity and inspired me to do the research that lead me to create Vintage Black Glamour.

My friends were wildly enthusiastic from the beginning and kind enough to talk me off the ledge when necessary: Tayari Jones, Aliah Greene, Patrice Grell Yursik, Jamyla Bennu, Monica Mingo, Denitria Lewis, Malaika Kebede, Jen Wang, Luvvie Ajaye, Rebecca Walker, Ernessa T. Carter, Dennis Dortch, Thembisa Mshaka, Nicole Blades, Helena Andrews, Zenobia Morrow, Veronica Marche-Miller, Kirsten Magwood, Tia Williams, Mayka Mei, Kellee Knighten Hough, Nyree Amory, Lyneka Little, Zaira Zafra, Mimi Mmabatho Selemela, Sherri Daye Scott, Sara Alloy, Nichelle Stephens and Merv Keizer.

A'Lelia Bundles, Farah Jasmine Griffin, Noliwe Rooks, Barbara Summers, Evie Shockley and Nichelle Tramble Spellman were kind enough to give me a lot of great advice and answer many, many questions for me. Nikki Giovanni and Pearl Cleage graciously allowed me to use a small portion of their work to illuminate my own and I am very grateful.

My cousin Kyle Taylor was the first to say to me, "Yes! That's the one!" when I told him that I was writing a book called Vintage Black Glamour. My sisters Tuwana Gainer and Charrell Cooper are probably looking for their names right about now so… yes, thank you my sisters. Family members who came through for me when it counted: my mother, Gail Parson Cooper and my stepmother Marsha Bennett Gainer. Friends who came through for me when it counted: Nicole LaMons and Delenia McIver. Asake Bomani, Queenesther James, Harold Morrison and Donna Monifa Jackson were bright and early with their enthusiasm and Dr. Bert Petersen has also been a true believer.

The staff at the Schomburg Center for Research in Black Culture at the New York Public Library led by Mary Yearwood was invaluable. Thank you Antony Toussaint, Michael Merry, Thomas Lisanti and Linden Anderson. The librarians at the F.D. Bluford Library at North Carolina A&T State University were extremely helpful in the earliest stages of the book as I researched Margaret Tynes. I would also like to thank the staffs at every institution and agency that assisted us with securing photos for this book.

Unwavering gratitude to Mal Peachey, John Conway, Michael Gray, Russell Beecher and the team at Essential Works and Rocket 88 Books for their hard work, dedication and patience.

Thank you to the loyal, engaged fans on Vintage Black Glamour's Facebook fan page, Twitter, Pinterest and Instagram for sharing, sharing, sharing! Your overwhelming ardor is the reason this book is now in your hands.